The PeopleWise Putting Strategic Plan

VISION

Every Golfer Can't Wait to Putt

MISSION

Lower the National Average Handicap of
American Golfers by 2010

GOALS

· Simplify the Mechanics of Putting

· Explain the Basics of the Mental Aspects of Putting

· Determine Individual Learning Preferences on
How to Best Master Putting Technique

· Diagnose How Individuals Develop
Olympian Focus and Confidence

· Provide a Feedback System to Determine
Improvement and Proficiency in Putting

ULTIMATE GOAL

Demystify Putting so it can be Mastered by Every Golfer

PEOPLEWISE®

putting

Get your brain in the game

written by

Dr. James S. Payne
and Larry W. Wagster

PeopleWise® Putting, is the second
book in the PeopleWise® Series

CYNTOMedia
CORPORATION

Pittsburgh, PA

SterlingHouse Publisher, Inc.

ISBN 1-58501-091-X

Trade Paperback
© Copyright 2005
Dr. James S. Payne and Larry W. Wagster
All Rights Reserved
First Printing — 2005
Library of Congress #2005922897

Request for information should be addressed to:

SterlingHouse Publisher, Inc.
7436 Washington Avenue
Pittsburgh, PA 15218
www.sterlinghousepublisher.com

SterlingHouse Publisher, Inc. is a company
of the CyntoMedia Corporation.

Cover Design: Jonah Lloyd
Typesetting & Layout Design: Beth Buckholtz

Printed in the United States of America

Dedicated to

Margaret McCausland
Master Teacher

*"When you have something to say
put it in writing for all to benefit from.
And don't use split infinitives."*

Margaret McCausland, 1962

Recognition

PeopleWise® Putting exists in book form because of the hard work and effort by:

Jennifer Piemme, my agent who saw a bit of talent in me and had faith in the concept of PeopleWise.®

Cindy Sterling, my publisher, who took a risk and put PeopleWise® on the market.

Jason Henze, production manager, who kept everything rolling.

Jonah Lloyd, art director, who designed the cover and format for PeopleWise® Putting .

Jennifer Brozak, proofreader, who helped make the book flow and reader-friendly,

And lastly,

Kimberly Simmons and **Ashley Brookshire**, typists, confidants, critics, and advisors, who made this project become a reality.

Acknowledgements

This work could not have been possible without the active involvement of the real golfers in our lives who regularly play on the weekends regardless of the weather. They come ready to play with sore muscles, backaches, foot problems, asthma, sinus headaches, and hemorrhoid malfunctions. They seldom practice, but they are good. They know who they are, and they are not trying to be someone else. They would rather play golf than watch golf although they all subscribe to the Golf Channel.

When one goes to the hospital for a repair job, they all visit unless it is on the weekend. They respect and admire each other. They help each other, but they don't want the other to win. On occasion they might say, "nice shot," but they know it was luck because they play so regularly, so consistently, that they know what each will do on each shot of each hole before they do it.

They are not much to look at from the outside, but they are pure on the inside. They have integrity and principles, but you better keep your eye on them because they have been known to cheat.

Each of these weekend Trojans has their own unique putting style, stance, and theory but what they all have in common is they are mentally tough. In alphabetical order, a special thanks goes to: Alan, Buddy, Bull, Danny, Don, Doug, George, Jay, Joe, Knox, Lewis, Scoop, Tom, Winfred, and Wrecker.

From the Mind of

[signature: Jim Payne]

8/17/09

Peter

   Hope you find PeopleWise
of continued interest related
to Graves.

   Thank you so much for your
email

     Best

            Jim

Read pp 119–125

Table of Contents

Read This First

The best thing that ever happened to my golf game was Larry Wagster, former golf coach at the University of Mississippi. Larry, at 64 years of age, has a registered handicap of five and is an excellent putter.

I learned to play golf as a psychology major taking a one hour credit course at Washburn University in Topeka, Kansas during my junior year in 1961. Because of my school work and later my professional career, I never had time to practice but enjoyed the game on weekends.

For years, my handicap fluctuated in the high teens until I met Larry. With minimal instruction and not much practice, my handicap dropped immediately into the single digits. How could this happen in such a brief period of time with minimal practice? Simple. Larry taught me how to putt.

Putting makes up approximately 43 percent of the game but few golfers master it. Larry taught me a few tricks, and the putts started dropping. Upon reaching sixty years of age, I became a student of putting by reading, watching videotapes, and attending a lot of golf clinics. I asked Larry to help me put what I had learned with what he knew into a training package that would help others master the art of putting. He agreed and one of the outcomes from this joint venture is the book you hold in your hands, *PeopleWise® Putting*.

PeopleWise® Putting is the second book in the PeopleWise® Series. The term PeopleWise® is an official trademark issued to me in 2001 by the United States Patent Office. PeopleWise® refers to people becoming wise about themselves and others. Individuals who become PeopleWise® know what makes them tick and how to tick better. *PeopleWise® Putting* teaches what you need to know to putt better and how to do it by knowing the way you learn best.

PeopleWise® Putting boils down the vast and sometimes overwhelming material on the mechanics of putting into fewer than ten pages. Larry and I have separated the proverbial wheat from the chaff. We have removed all the confusing, irrelevant stuff and retained only the important stuff that directly and dramatically effects putting. The great philosopher Pareto purports that 80 percent of the value is usually in 20 percent of the time. The 80/20 rule suggests that in a list of ten items, doing two of them will yield most (80%) of the value. *PeopleWise® Putting* gives you the 20 percent in a fast read, easy to understand ten pages that produce over 80 percent of what is important. The ten pages can be read in fifteen minutes after which you will know all you need to know about the mechanics of putting. Unfortunately putting is mostly mental. Once you develop a smooth and consistent stroke, the rest is mental.

All of the knowledge related to the mental part of putting is based on the works of three motivational experts: Maxwell Maltz (*Psycho-Cybernetics*), Dennis Waitley (*Seeds of Greatness*), and Louis Tice (*A Better World, A Better You*). Their contributions are referred to in golfing circles as visual imagery and mental rehearsal. Larry and I have taken their combined 769 pages from their three seminal works along with the important teachings of countless others and condensed it into thirty pages. Here you learn everything you need to know about the mental side in about forty-five minutes.

Now you can consume these forty pages in sixty minutes and you could go out and practice and become good, in fact real good, but if you are the average golfer you can't and won't. You can't because you have a life. You have obligations. You have chores to do. You won't because practicing putting is boring. There are a lot of things in your life that are more important and more fun than putting.

But the good news is you don't have to practice hours on end to get good. Why? Because you have the physical ability and the intelligence to do it.

Let's face it, it doesn't take strength, agility, quickness, flexibility, speed or anything physical to be a good putter. It takes more energy to get to the ball than it does to stroke it. The movements and energy used by your hands to stroke the ball is less than it is to feed your face from plate to mouth.

Stroking the putt doesn't require great intellect; it is not complicated. It is about as simple as walking and most certainly simpler than skipping. So what is the problem? The problem is not everyone learns the same way, and every instructional book assumes any learner will and can learn from their proposed system, technique, and/or program. One interesting exception is Chuck Hogan, creator of Sports Enhancement Associates. His unique approach identifies specific learning styles through personality types and neurolinguistics. James Bartlett lists him as one of golf's most unusual instructors in his book *Golf Gurus: The Wisdom of the Game's Greatest Instructors*. Any golfer will find Chuck Hogan's work refreshing and useful.

There are many excellent instructional books on putting, but *PeopleWise® Putting* is the only one that takes into account the recent findings of brain technology. Brain technology is so new that 90 percent of all neurologists are alive today. We have learned more about the brain in the past five years than in the past one hundred. Because of philosophers and theorists like Clare Graves (*Levels of Psychological Existence*), and Mihaly Czikszentmihalyi (*Finding Flow in Everyday Life*), and brain researchers like Amy Haufler, Bradley Hatfield, Marian Diamond, Ronald Kotulak, Daniel Goleman, and Joseph LeDoux, we know that emotion plays a significant part in performance and that the activation of the brain plays a major role in how we learn. What we know today that we didn't know before is anyone can regulate their emotion and learn how to activate their own brain to attain the confidence that leads to Olympian focus. *PeopleWise® Putting* devotes the remaining pages of this book to teaching you how to learn to putt. You will assess how, where, and the intensity of the activation of your own brain, how to use it to improve your own putting; and you will know what to do and how to stroke the ball without hours and hours of practice. The beauty is in its simplicity.

You have the ability and the intelligence to be a good putter. Now you have in your hands the secret to actually doing it.

This book approaches putting from the vantage point of a right-hander, that is, the player stands on the left side of the ball. If you are a left-hander and putt from what some writers refer to as the deviant side, just reverse the information and make the appropriate adjustments.

The development and ultimately the completion of this book was truly collaborative. Larry was instrumental in correcting my mistakes as a putter as well as a writer. Occasionally a first person "I" will pop up. This refers to me and is used to illustrate a personal situation or belief for which the use of "we" would not only be awkward, it would be inaccurate.

The last four chapters are adaptations from the first book in the PeopleWise® Series, *PeopleWise® Brain to Brain*. These chapters have been modified to directly address putting. For individuals interested in knowing more about the theories, principles and techniques of PeopleWise® they may wish to consult *PeopleWise® Brain to Brain*. Also there is a Definition of Terms section in the rear of the book for beginning golfers that may not be familiar with terms specifically related to golf.

Here are some interesting numbers:

- There are thirty million golfers in the United States (Miller 1996, p. 17).

- There are one hundred million golfers in the world (Miller 1996, p. 58).

- There are 16,743 golf courses in the United States (Payne 2003, p. 7).

- The scores of golfers are not improving.
  The handicap of the average American golfer is stagnant (Gallwey 1998, p. XVI).

- Less than one percent of all golfers have completed a round of golf in par or better (Parent 2002, p. 10).

- Three million new golfers are introduced to the game each year while another three million give up (Payne 2003, p. 8).

The bottom line is Larry and I, in this joint effort, want you to become a PeopleWise® putter and master this very important part of the game. And by doing so you and many others will positively affect the numbers presented above. Golf is too good a game to let putting get you down.

> James S. Payne
> Professor, University of Mississippi,
> Fulbright Scholar and
> Putting Sage

CHAPTER 1
It Ain't Rocket Science

The purpose of this book is to improve your putting and ultimately lower your golf score, period. You don't need a NASA engineer to tell you how to sink a four foot putt. It ain't rocket science.

Enjoyment: If you are looking for a way to enjoy the game of golf more, then return this book for a full refund. This book is about putting and putting ain't fun. If you want enjoyment from golf, you may want to consider going to the nineteenth hole for a drink of something warm or warming. Or if you are looking for enjoyment that borders on ecstasy, wrap yourself around a peyote button or two and read *Golf in the Kingdom* by Michael Murphy. It is an enjoyable read.

Recreation: If you want the game to be something other than what it is, like recreation, you may want to take up camping, canoeing, sailing, or go on a picnic. Don't waste your time with golf let alone putting.

> I was in Savannah, Georgia and had time to drive to Hilton Head for a round of golf. I was paired with this guy that thought golf was a recreational event. I think he was trying to do some type of self-discovery thing. I knew I was in for an exceptionally trying round when I had to keep reminding him to hit the ball. We would proceed down the fairway and he would continually walk past his ball. He was caught up in the beauty of the surroundings, the smell in the air, the enlightenment of the sunrays … the ambience so to speak. By the seventh hole, I verbally knocked all that nonsense out of him real quick and played the back nine by myself.

Oneness with the Universe: If you seek something mystical or want to explore the Fourth Dimension, forget it. This book is written on real paper not stone. It was not channeled. This book is for people in this three dimensional world with their feet firmly planted on the ground.

Self-awareness: If you don't know who you are or where you are, this book won't help. This book will only help those that can get to the golf course, load the clubs in the cart and get to the first tee unassisted.

Health Benefits: We are talking putting here not racquetball.

Sportsmanship and camaraderie: This book is about improving your own putting, not your playing companions. Bonding in golf is a little too...intimate. You will not find bonding directly or indirectly addressed in this book.

Literary Gem: This book is not a classic nor will it ever be a classic. It is not a novel nor does it try to teach an important lesson about life. This book will not expand your thinking nor will it provoke higher level questions. For a real mind blower try *Golf for Enlightenment* by Deepak Chopra. It is a great read. However, this book you hold in your hand, is about putting.

Humor: If you find anything that makes you grin or smile, it is not because of anything intended in this book. Possibly it could be because you may possess a tinge of perverted humor in your soul.

Love: Don't even think about it. Love has nothing to do with putting. We don't understand love. We don't want to understand love, and you won't find love in this book.

This book is for real golfers. Real people you have never heard of, but know. People like Alan Tidwell, Wrecker Thornton, Bull Collier, Joe Larson, Buddy Gresham, and Don Shaver.

Don't get the idea this book is gender specific. According to Larry Miller in his book *Golfing in the Zone*, for the last three years,

60 percent of all new golfers are women. And it is important to add they buy books too. So we are writing for people like Kimberly Sue Simmons, Janet Lou Purdy, Cindy Sterling, Felisa Redmond, Tippa Clark, and Flippa Rose.

However, this book is for all those real golfers that haven't given up their day jobs. It is for those that golf on the weekends and don't have time to practice except for hitting a bucket of balls now and then and throwing three or four balls down on the practice green and knocking them around for five to ten minutes while waiting for their tee time.

These are the real golfers who not only do not have time to practice, they believe practice is cheating. Anyone can master any sport if you have time to practice, but the real challenge in life is to get real good without practice. That is what this book is about. How to get real good at putting with minimal practice.

Here is something to think about. Dave Pelz (2000), believed by many to be the foremost authority on putting, believes only one out of ten people actually improve their putting when they practice, 40 percent show no change while the remaining 50 percent actually get worse (p. 217). Real golfers can add, subtract, multiply, and divide and they don't like the odds. As you master PeopleWise® Putting, what little practice you do is so focused and tailored to your individual needs and disposition, you will experience improvement immediately. It is the true optimization of your effort. You accomplish more in less time.

The objective of putting is simple enough. Knock a 1.68-inch in diameter ball into a 4.25-inch wide hole with an instrument known as a putter. All balls and holes are the same size but putters come in all shapes, sizes, lengths, and weights. Many a real golfer thinks the putter is the key to good putting. Here's some news for you. The key is the person holding the putter. In the first book of the PeopleWise® series, *PeopleWise® Brain to Brain*, a story is told about Lee Trevino.

On September 15, 2001, during a conversation with Lane Vines, golf pro, Grand Oaks Country Club, Oxford, Mississippi, he reported that one time Lee Trevino, golfing great, studied an eight-foot putt on the last hole. He was with his friends and had a small wager on the side. He needed this putt to win. The ball was struck, a crisp ping resounded through the air, followed by a plop as the ball fell into the bottom of the cup. Lee Trevino smiled, pumped his fists triumphantly into the air, while his opponents shook their heads in disbelief. It's not so spectacular that he made the putt, what made it great is he tapped it in with a Dr. Pepper bottle. Rumor has it that on many occasions he putted with Dr. Pepper bottles. Is it any wonder that later in his career, Dr. Pepper became one of his major sponsors? (pp. 4 & 5)

The putter is the instrument of choice used by the real golfers of this land but the person holding the putter is far more important. Dave Pelz, putting guru, in his book *Dave Pelz's Putting Bible*, writes:

The best putters of our time — from George Archer and Dave Stockton, through Ben Crenshaw, Loren Roberts, Greg Norman, and Brad Faxon, to Lee Janzen, the late Payne Stewart, and now David Duval and Brent Geiberger — could putt well with just about any putter. This is because each one had developed great putting skills and strokes that they grooved and own. No matter what putter you hand them, whether it fit them or not, they could use their own stroke and succeed. (p. 242)

Getting back to Lee Trevino, Dave Pelz mentions that Lee Trevino won the 1972 British Open, at Muirfield in Scotland, with a putter he found in a used-club barrel. Lee credited his win to the putter but Pelz is quick to point out Lee had a smooth-as-silk stroke.

Joseph Parent in *Zen Golf* mentions a player in Qualifying school who missed three consecutive three-foot putts on the first three holes. Being three over after three holes he lost his temper and snapped his putter over his knee. For the rest of the round, he putted with his driver. "...over the next fifteen holes, he made only one bogey, sank several par-saving putts, and rolled in five birdies to finish at 71, one under par for the round" (p. 92). Dr. Parent goes on to explain that putting with his driver forced him to pay full attention to the process of keeping the face of the club square on line and putting a good stroke on the ball.

Although the person holding the putter is the most important thing, having a putter you feel comfortable with is of some importance. Obviously, if you don't feel comfortable with your putter, you won't feel comfortable putting. Peter Dobereiner, author of *Golf a la Cart*, shares the deteriorating relationship between Mark Jones and his putter after a first round of the Bob Hope Benefit Classic when he kicked the putter all around the car park and then threw it into a bush, saying "You can stay there all night and we'll see if that teaches you how to behave" (p. 56).

Patrick Cohn and Robert Winters, in *The Mental Art of Putting* mention, "one thing is certain, no matter what putter you use, if you can have success with it, the putter starts to look good" (p. 39). They go on to mention that some good putters develop a trust in a putter that they tend to treasure. They even go so far as to name their magical putters. Some of the most notable ones are: Ben Crenshaw's "Little Ben," Arnold Palmer's "Old Faithful," Paul Runyan's "Little Poison," and perhaps the most famous putter, Bobby Jones' "Calamity Jane."

As you know, the putter is not magic. The real magic happens when everything is in sync, and the ball goes in the hole.

CHAPTER 2
Two Rivers

When the command module, Kitty Hawk, landed on the moon many of us watched, live on television, in the comfort of our own homes, Alan Shepard hit a shot a country mile with a six iron no less. Maybe it was his passion, as is every golfer's passion, to hit a shot that would never come down. But take notice, he didn't pull out a putter to putt the first ball on another planetary body. Putting ain't exciting.

Michael Murphy (1972) makes a salient point, "Hogan for one has sometimes said that putting should be abandoned, that it ruins an otherwise exciting game" (p. 162).

Patrick Cohn and Robert Winters (1995) mention, while putting, the ball is never airborne. They conclude putting is a game within a game. Some call it a black art, a mystic science, or an exercise in human patience. They go on to quote Curtis Strange (1990) PGA Tour, "Putting, to me, takes more guts than any other part of the game because it's mostly mental, requiring little physical ability" (p. xvi). "Most great putters, including Jack Nicklaus, agree that putting is 2 percent mechanics and 98 percent confidence and touch" (p. xvi). Furthermore, according to Jack Nicklaus, "Undoubtedly, the majority of present-day tournaments are decided on the putting surface" (p. xvii).

When you review the literature on putting, it becomes apparent more pages are devoted to the mechanics of putting than to the mental aspects. The mechanics of putting have been analyzed, studied, inspected, and dissected down to the point of determining the balance of the individual golf ball. Every training device imaginable has been placed on the market to help the average golfer become a better putter. Putting rails, tracks, and guides are sold everyday. Different types of indoor putting greens and cups that send the ball scooting back are available. Laser beams, string, tape, and various types of cords that help line up a putt are abundant. Yet, with all these training devices for putting and all the voluminous material on how to putt, most people agree putting is mostly mental.

For a peek at the many training devices available you may consult Bill Hogan's, *Golf Gadgets*, but we don't recommend it. We believe that most training devices are a bad investment in both time and money. Later, this book will show you how to get the greatest benefit from training aides by using an eight foot piece of fishing line, two eye hooks, and a pocket mirror. Maximum benefit with minimal practice is what PeopleWise® Putting is all about.

There is also some stuff written on the mental part, but it is dramatically dwarfed by the mechanical stuff. When you tease out everything written about visual imagery and mental rehearsal, what is left related to the mental aspect of the game is very sparse to say the least. So what presently exists is an over abundance of information on the mechanics of putting with a little bit on visual imagery and mental rehearsal. What is left over wouldn't fill a thimble.

W. Timothy Gallwey in his best selling book, *The Inner Game of Golf* (Revised Edition), explains this duality of mechanics versus the mental part by referring to it as the river of "formulas" and the river of "feel." The "formulas" part has been a favorite subject of inquiry for the Newtonian mind. "This appetite stems from the same quest that fueled the technological Newtonian revolution: the desire to know and control" (p. xii). The "feel" side referred to as the "mental side" or "inner game" doesn't get as much attention as the "formulas" side because it is hard to see and impossible to objectively measure. "So these two streams, formulas and feelings, have moved through history as two great rivers, one seeming to swell as the other ebbs, sometimes crossing each other but rarely joining" (p. xiii).

After reviewing the literature on putting, we have concluded it is more like one giant mechanics river and a very small mental stream that are separated much like science and art. You can't measure art although you can study it, appreciate it, and to some degree teach it. The mental side of putting can be taught. In other words, confidence can be acquired to the point of gaining Olympian focus.

By applying visual imagery and mental rehearsal strategies, confidence can be learned. Furthermore, by utilizing state-of-the-art brain technology that has been recently unveiled with tried and true visual imagery and mental rehearsal, Olympian focus can be experienced on demand by anyone at anytime without equipment. Confidence leading to Olympian focus will improve your putting overnight with minimal practice.

Why is it that sometimes the hole looks the size of a bucket, and at other times it is the size of a jigger? It is because the size of the cup grows in relationship to your confidence. The more confident you are, the bigger the hole. The more doubt you have, the more the hole shrinks to the point of a pinhead. According to Parent (2002), Bobby Locke, one of the all-time great putters, said, "Approaching a putt with doubt in your mind is nearly always fatal" (p. 46).

Take a golf ball and toss it into the air about a foot high and catch it. Do this two or three times. Now toss it about three feet and catch it. Do this two or three times. Notice you were able to do it successfully without consciously thinking. The reason you can do this is because the subconscious part of your brain communicates to your muscles and nervous system what to do automatically in order to catch the ball.

Now throw the ball up and catch it again but this time tell yourself to keep your eyes on the ball all the way to your receiving hand. Notice you can do it and if you continue, pretty soon keeping your eyes on the ball will become automatic without consciously thinking or reminding yourself to do it. In other words, you have taught yourself consciously to keep your eyes on the ball and now you do it without thinking. Keeping your eyes on the ball has increased your skill level.

The same is true when you tie your shoelaces. Now you do it automatically without thinking, but at first you had to be taught.

This is exactly what happens with learning how to putt. Eventually the stroke must become automatic.

Gallwey (1998) mentions that the best putter on the 1996 Tour was Brad Faxon. When asked for advice about putting, he was quoted in *Golf* magazine as saying, "Believe it or not, I'm not really thinking about anything when I putt...It's hard to teach. I let my instincts take over...When I'm putting well, I feel as if I can make everything" (Gallwey, 1998, p. 102).

So to become a good putter you will, in the beginning, use the conscious part of your brain by teaching yourself the mechanics while still incorporating the subconscious part of the brain to coordinate your muscles and nervous system. You not only need both mechanics and the mental part to become good, the mechanics and mental part must join or blend and become inseparable.

Now put a ball down on a level putting green at a distance you can make ten times out of ten tries, say two-to two-and-a-half feet from the hole. As you stroke the ball notice how confident and relaxed you are. Now, at this same distance, instead of striking the ball on the center of the clubface, hit it on the toe of the clubface. Notice you still make the putts. Why? Because your subconscious automatically self-adjusted your muscles and compensated for the difference of hitting the ball on the toe as opposed to the center of the clubface without you having to consciously think about it.

Now, at the same distance, as you pull the putter back, move it during the back stroke at least three inches outside your usual back swing path (either right or left) then stroke the ball. Notice you continuously made the putts, or if at first you missed, on subsequent strokes you somehow quickly adjusted to make the ball go in the hole. How can this be? You violated the mechanics of the game by physically doing what you know you are not supposed to do yet you could still get the ball in the hole. This shows the power of your subconscious and its ability to self-correct.

At this short distance, there is a lot of room for error, and your confidence level is so high and you are so relaxed the cup is mentally the size of a bucket. At this distance, you can slap it in one handed while simultaneously stepping toward the hole to pick the ball out of the cup. Although rare, we have even seen professionals do it on television in major tournaments.

Many a weekend golfer will pick these short putts up as a "gimmie" and add a stroke to their score assuming they can automatically make it without trying. This decreases playing time and probably on occasion improves a score or two especially if the putt is not on level ground. A "gimmie" is determined by the putt being within the leather. Within the leather refers to the ball being within the distance of the metal part of the shaft. When the putt is close to being outside this safe distance of the "gimmie" the player puts the putter club head in the hole and uses the shaft as a crude tape measure. If the ball lies within the steel part of the shaft it qualifies as a "gimmie"; however, if the ball touches the grip or as they say leather (grips used to be wrapped in leather straps) the ball must be putted.

> Wrecker Thornton developed a way to quickly improve anyone's putting over night. Wrecker is eighty-two years old, holds an unofficial handicap of 15, continues to work during the week at the local body shop repairing damaged cars, has had two heart by-passes, three angioplasties, pulls his own golf cart on a trailer behind his 1982 Ford F100 pick-up, and dresses as his name implies. Wrecker Thornton is a real golfer. He golfs every weekend — rain, sunshine, snow or hail. He is almost impossible to beat on a freezing day when the flaps on his hunting cap are down and securely tied under his chin. Wrecker can putt wearing galoshes and mittens.

> Wrecker found he could take his pocketknife and remove about four inches off the lower part of his grip on his putter and improve his putting overnight. We all thought this was cheating but we

could not find it to be illegal in the USGA Official Rule Book. In fact, we couldn't even find the word "gimmie" in it.

It took us a couple of weekends of arguing but the situation was resolved by everyone in the group using Wrecker's putter to measure their own "gimmies." Everyone loves Wrecker and appreciates his contribution to the art of putting, but no one wants him to win.

PeopleWise® Putting does not include the Thornton pocket-knife putter grip development as part of its program for improving putting. But if your opponent uses it, you may want to consider using it too. In the circles of real golfers, it *is* legal regardless of what the USGA Rule Book says.

However, an important lesson to be learned from actually putting "gimmies" is once the conscious part of the brain communicates to the subconscious exactly what the goal or target is, the subconscious automatically self-adjusts and compensates for any minor error in the stroke. Thus "gimmies" for the most part need not be putted.

The subconscious is powerful, but the purpose of perfecting the mechanics is so the subconscious doesn't have to work so hard. Once you get your stroke down at a reasonable skill level, the subconscious won't have to work so hard self-correcting. It is impossible to stroke the ball exactly the same every time, but when you get the mechanics down you get real close to duplicating the skill. Soon you can repeat the stroke without thinking, just like tying your shoelaces.

The secret to learning the mechanics is to get the fundamentals exactly right without complicating it so much that the subconscious can't take over. Work on what is important and keep it simple.

CHAPTER 3
Nuts and Bolts

Here are the nuts and bolts, the scoop, the skinny, on the mechanics of putting. You only need to know three things: keep your head still, hit the ball on the sweet spot, and use a smooth stroke that keeps the putter head square to the aimline.[1] If you learn to do these three basic things consistently without consciously thinking, your subconscious will take care of the rest.

What about reading the greens? The real golfer is smart enough to figure out downhill putts go faster than uphill putts. On undulating greens where the green is sloped to the left the ball will move left, and furthermore, the distance the ball moves left is directly proportional to the steepness of the slope. The ball moves faster on shorter grass than longer grass, and the ball may sometimes move slightly in the direction of the grain of the grass if you can ever see it. Even though reading greens is a no brainer for the real golfer, it will be covered in detail in the next chapter, Too Much.

What about the lumpy donut? Dave Pelz (2000) made an interesting observation that golfers seldom step inside a six-inch radius of the hole. Thus as the day wears on with more and more play on the greens a thin flat donut is formed where the players step while leaving a slight ramp or raised area in the grass around the cup where no one steps (pp. 19-21). Pelz even counted the number of steps a foursome makes on each green to be more than five hundred. He did this by counting the footprints left by the first foursome to play a green that had dew on the grass. Pretty clever.

---

[1]Aimline — The initial line that the ball is intended to start on. It is a straight line used as a guide or sight. The aimline extends both behind the ball and past the hole. A break is the distance between the aimline and the cup. For instance if there is a two-inch break to the left, the ball will move two inches left from the point of contact to the ball dropping in the hole.

I took a group of real golfers and gave them each a ruler and had them measure the length of the grass next to the cup and measure the length of the grass a putter's length from the cup, just beyond the "gimmie" range. I had them measure once in the morning, once at noon, and once in the late afternoon. I averaged their scores and found no real measurable difference between the distances and the times the measurements were taken. I also had each one putt five balls four feet from the cup and record their results. Again no differences were found in the group average scores from morning, noon, and late afternoon. But it needs to be noted two of the subjects couldn't participate in the late afternoon because they had to go home and take a nap. Now granted, the rulers only measured things within one thirty second of an inch and the sample used were real golfers that were good putters, not mathematicians. But after I told them why I was conducting the study their collective wisdom registered a common sense fact that is worth passing on. "If you can't see it with the naked eye then it probably won't effect the putt all that much."

A case can be made that unseeable factors affect putts. Every real golfer on any given day has hit the perfect putt that didn't go in because of an unseen spike mark or imperfection in the green. However, just as many putts on a given day that were off line and should not have gone in, actually drop in the hole because of an imperfection in the green. In the long run it averages out. According to Parent (2002), "Golf and life aren't fair on a day to day basis. But those good and bad breaks even out over the long run" (p. 13). Since the ball never leaves the ground, you can't control Mother Nature, but you can control your stroke.

Right now let's don't think about anything other than head still, sweet spot, and smooth stroke. Other things will be covered later if you really want to know even though they are irrelevant to improving your putting.

Head Still: It is best to keep your head still during the stroking of the putt because the less movement of the head the less complicated the stroke, the less complicated the stroke, the less your subconscious has to work. Here is how you learn to keep your head still.

Stand any way you want in any position you want, but position your head immediately above the back edge of the ball. About the position of having your left eye directly over the ball. Most good golfers can do this without any help or assistance. However, if you are not sure of your head placement being directly above the back of the ball you need not plumb bob your forehead, eyes, or nose. Just take a pocket mirror and place it on the ground under the rear of the ball and adjust your head so you can see your eyes.

Once you get set up with your head immediately above the back of the ball, then you are ready to stroke the putt. While stroking the putt keep your head down, and continuously look where the back of the ball is and was.

Within a short period of time with very little practice you can do this without thinking. Just like in other sports, you learn to keep your eyes on a moving ball. Actually, it is easier to learn to keep your head still than it is to keep your eyes on a moving ball. Keeping your head still is important to being a good putter because it simplifies your stroke, so your subconscious doesn't have to adjust, readjust, and self-correct your muscles.

If for some reason you can't keep your head still, try using Tim Gallwey's (1998) inner golf awareness technique of not trying to hold your head still but instead develop a sense of awareness of where your head is and what it is doing during the set up and while stroking the putt. By being aware and sensitive to the position of your head, you will automatically begin to keep it still without forcing yourself consciously to do it. This is a good technique, especially for golfers who are reflective thinkers whose brain activates in the frontal region. At this time don't worry about what type of thinker you are or what your brain does or does not do. Just learn to teach yourself to place your head directly above the rear of the ball, and keep it still while stroking the putt.

Sweet Spot: Every putter head has a sweet spot. When you hit the ball on the sweet spot, the putter will not twist in your hands. When your putter does not twist in your hands, the subconscious does not have to readjust and compensate for the shot.

Not all putters have the sweet spot accurately located. It is important to know where the sweet spot is and mark it accordingly. To determine the sweet spot, hold the very end of the grip between the thumb and fingers of an outstretched arm directly in front of you. Place the putter head parallel to your body. Let gravity dangle the club straight down. Now, slightly adjust the shaft so the sole of the putter head is parallel to the ground. For most putters the angle is about 70 degrees. This is the angle the shaft is when you putt. Take a coin between the thumb and forefinger of the remaining hand, and strike the face of the putter head with the edge of the coin hard enough to make the putter head swing away from you two to three inches. First strike the putter head toward the toe, and you will feel it twist in your fingers. Imagine what your subconscious mind has to communicate to your muscles and nervous system to compensate for this wobbliness to make the ball go where it is supposed to go. Now with the edge of the coin strike the putter head toward the heel. Again feel it twist in the fingers of your out stretched hand. Every time the putter head strikes the ball out of the sweet spot the putter head twists making the subconscious have to unnecessarily work to get the muscles to move the ball in the right direction. The farther the ball is from the sweet spot, the more the twist; the more the twist, the more the subconscious has to realign and self-correct.

Now strike the putter head with the coin multiple times, moving the coin toward the center of the clubface. As the coin strikes closer to the sweet spot, the less the twist. When the coin strikes the sweet spot, the club head will bounce straight back with no twist whatsoever. Also it will bounce back with greater force. When the putter head strikes the ball on the sweet spot, it immediately goes straight on line. If the swing is on the aimline, the putter head is square, and the ball is struck on the sweet spot, the ball will roll true in the intended direction. When this happens, the subconscious doesn't have to do much.

Once you find the sweet spot, mark the top edge of the putter head with a permanent marker or scratch it in with a metal saw blade or file. "If necessary paint it in a color that is easily visible" (Andrisani, 1998, p. 124). Note: most putters are mass-produced, and if they have a line or dot on the top edge of the putter head it may not be exactly where the sweet spot is. All good golfers check to make sure where the sweet spot is on their particular putter.

Now you begin to stroke the ball on the sweet spot with your head kept still. When you do this, the subconscious doesn't have to perform a lot of mental gymnastics to get the ball to go on its intended course. Most real golfers do not have any trouble striking the ball on the sweet spot once the sweet spot is located and marked accordingly. However, as explained in the previous section on keeping your head still, if you experience trouble, try using the awareness technique. Don't try to hit the ball on the sweet spot. Instead, focus your awareness on where the putter head hits the ball. This will be surprisingly easy because every time the ball is struck away from the sweet spot the putter will ever so slightly twist in your hands.

Once you are aware of the importance of the sweet spot, you will know immediately when you hit it right. When you hit it right, it feels great, and the sound of the putter head striking the ball gives out a crisp, clean ping. When the sweet spot is missed it feels ugly and gives out a terrible thud. Gallwey (1998) relates a story of the blind golfer who was playing with a foursome. When one of the blind player's opponents left a sixteen-foot putt five feet short, he remarked, "That is about the worst putt I ever heard" (p. 112).

Soon you will be striking the ball on the sweet spot naturally without thinking or trying and it will feel so pure and sound so beautiful. When you are able to stroke the ball automatically without consciously thinking while keeping your head still and hitting it every time on the sweet spot, you are ready to develop a smooth-as-silk stroke.

Smooth Stroke: The easiest way to putt the ball straight is to place the ball on the ground between your legs, hold the putter head square to the aimline and stroke it like a croquet mallet. When using this stroke, your eyes are parallel to the ground, giving you maximum vision of the putt. The putter hangs down between your legs, and the swing forms a natural arc, using a pendulum motion, which requires the least amount of body and muscle movement. But when the legendary Sam Snead used this technique in professional play, the USGA Rule Commission immediately ruled it illegal.

Since it is illegal to straddle the ball the next easiest way to putt is to use a long-shafted putter. The end of the long-shafted putter is held stationary against your chest or chin with one hand while the other hand moves the club in a natural arc, pendulum motion with minimal body movement. If you are not already using a traditional putter then at least try a long-shafted putter. It is superior to the standard one. But at this time most golfers have become accustomed to the standard putter and have developed a reasonable stroke. To them, the long-shafted putter feels awkward, and besides that it doesn't look right. Also, it doesn't fit well in your bag.

When using a standard putter, it is best to use a pendulum motion with the putter head square to the aimline and the path of the stroke from back swing to follow through being held on the aimline path. This approach uses the least amount of body and muscle movement, is the easiest to learn, and when executed correctly requires less for the subconscious to do.

18

Since you have mastered your head placement and you are hitting the ball on the sweet spot, the development of a smooth as silk stroke that minimizes body and muscular movement is well within your grasp.

Grip the club any way you want: left hand down — right hand up; right hand down — left hand up; both hands together; or both hands separated. The important thing is to hold the club as comfortably as you can while giving yourself reasonable control of the putter.

While holding the club, let your arms hang down naturally in front of you, and take a stance with your feet comfortably placed far enough from the ball that the sole of the putter head may be placed level on the ground directly behind the ball.

Some good putters slightly bend their knees, others keep their knees straight, some putt knock-kneed and a few bow-legged. The important thing is to form a solid foundation from which the club may swing in a pendulum motion.

With your head aligned correctly and stable, rotate your shoulders so the club head moves back and forth on the same path of the aimline. This is best done by tipping your shoulders as if on an axis, where the middle of your neck forms the apex of the arc. Most good golfers form a triangle between their hands and their two shoulders. They try to keep this triangle as the body tips the club in a pendulum motion while keeping the head completely still.

Always keep in mind: head still, sweet spot, smooth swing with putter head square to the aimline, and then stroke back and follow through on the aimline path using a pendulum motion.

After you get the pendulum motion down, for most golfers, the difficult thing is keeping the putter head square to the aimline and the swing path on line. Many devices have been developed to help master this seemingly simple task, but one device, an eight-foot fishing cord attached to two eyehooks seems superior.

If you have trouble keeping the putter head square and on line try stringing an eight-foot fishing line between two eyehooks. For best results, get eyehooks with shafts eight to nine inches in length, or you may use gutter spikes. Pick out a level spot on the practice green, and place one eye hook in the ground about an inch behind the hole while stringing the fishing line across the center of the cup. Place the other eyehook in the ground, so the fishing line is taut and about five inches in the air parallel to the ground.

Start out by placing the ball directly under the fishing line about two to three feet from the cup. As you address and stroke the ball, you will immediately sense exactly what is necessary to putt the ball straight on line. Using this device you immediately see the squareness of the putter head and the swing line path.

After using this device a few times you will quickly be able to move the ball farther back from the hole and still maintain a perfect pendulum stroke with the putter head square and swing path on line. The fishing line and two eyehooks system will get you putting the ball in the correct direction. Next you work on distance.

To minimize muscle movement, rather than swinging the club harder to get more distance, bring the putter head farther back on the back swing. Regardless of the distance desired the back swing and follow through should be approximately the same length. When using the pendulum stroke, the distance on the arc going back is the same as the continuing arc going forward. So rather than trying to muscle the ball on longer putts, you simply enlarge the distance of the arc. This allows you to have the same rhythm on every stroke regardless of distance.

So what you teach yourself to do mechanically to be a good putter is:

1. Place your head above the rear of the ball, and keep it still throughout the stroke.

2. Hit the ball on the sweet spot of the putter head.

3. Use a pendulum motion while keeping the head of the putter square to the aimline and the swing on the aimline path. Regulate the distance of the putt by adjusting the length of the arc using the same rhythm.

When you master these three techniques and do them consistently without thinking, you will be a good putter. The attainment of being classified as a good putter is when the weekend golfer putts on a level green at the average of what a professional, on tour golfer, putts on undulating greens. Dave Pelz (2000) has calculated the average of putts converted at varying distances of professional golfers on tour. The following are approximations taken from the Pelz data (p. 7) that you can use as a measure of your putting ability.

One foot	100 percent holed
Two feet	100 percent holed
Three feet	85 percent holed
Four feet	70 percent holed
Five feet	60 percent holed
Six feet	50 percent holed
Seven feet	40 percent holed
Eight feet	35 percent holed
Nine feet	25 percent holed
Ten feet	20 percent holed

The average weekend golfer will attain these averages with minimal practice as they master the basics detailed in this chapter. However, to reach these averages the three techniques must become automatic so the subconscious can devote itself to other more important things.

The next time you begin to putt and catch yourself consciously thinking about your head placement or the squareness of the putter head, or something about your pendulum swing, stop for a moment and reflect on the fact you do not have to consciously think about walking, tying your shoelaces, or feeding your face. Your mental frame of mind must be free from conscious thoughts while putting. It is of paramount importance that you master the putting basics to the point you don't and won't think about it while stroking the ball. According to Parent (2002), "If you are thinking about your swing, you're thinking, not swinging. Your mind is 'in your head' with conceptual ideas about how you should swing, rather than 'in your body', running the swing" (p. 91). While putting, do not let yourself get involved in mental chatter (Parent 2002, p. 66).

To move from being a good putter to being a real good putter, you need to master the mental part because once you master the mechanics the rest is mostly, if not entirely, mental. Logically the next chapter would begin to teach you about the mental part of putting, but for some reason many weekend golfers have an insatiable desire to know a lot of stuff about the mechanics of putting even though it doesn't help improve their stroke or score. Although real golfers are intelligent, many are illogical, and they all have needs. The next chapter is designed to fulfill those needs to know a lot of stuff that won't help your putting but are interesting to read.

CHAPTER 4
Too Much

Not all golfers are the same and there have been and are many excellent putters who have mastered the game using unique, unusual, and different techniques for getting the ball to roll in the hole. The previous chapter provided three fundamental mechanics for putting that minimizes the complexity of the stroke. The simpler the stroke, the more repeatable it is, and the less the subconscious has to work. This chapter covers aspects of putting that some players, writers, researchers, and theorists think are important. We believe no one single aspect covered in this chapter will significantly improve your putting but you may find something helpful that can be added to your present stroke and will be worth trying.

To give you an idea of the range of differences in putting consider the following: Bobby Locke put hook spin on many of his putts. Chi Chi Rodriguez cuts across his putts swinging from outside to inside the aimline. Gary Player pops his putts while Jack Nicklaus pushes his putter down the aimline. Arnold Palmer likes using his wrists followed by muscle power; Billy Casper uses his wrists predominantly to roll the putt while Tiger Woods uses his arms. Some of the pendulum stroke putters include Greg Norman, Loren Roberts, and Phil Mickelson. One thing for sure, to get good, you must commit to your stroke, groove it to the point it is repeatable and automatic and believe the ball is going to drop in the cup.

To begin you may want to check the ball.

Ball: Golf balls today are balanced and not out of round, but a little bit of mud or dirt can affect the roll. So mark your ball, pick it up and wipe it off good. If you want to check the roundness of the ball, there are devices, both metal and plastic, that have holes in them the exact size of the golf ball. Some are in the form of a golf ball ring that can be attached to your bag. They are used to determine if the ball is out of round.

To check the center of weight distribution or as some refer to it the center of gravity of the ball, there are devices that spin the ball allowing centrifugal force to locate the balance line. You can also float your ball in Epsom salts to achieve the same result. Either way, we don't believe it will help improve your putting, but marking a straight line on your ball might. Originally some players marked the balance line on their ball and then lined the balance line up with the aimline. This helps determine the direction of the intended putt. Determining the balance line may be a little bit of an overkill on the science of the mechanics of putting, but a sight line drawn on your ball with a permanent marker is not. Tiger Woods uses this technique to help him line up his putts, so it can't be all that bad.

Glove: Some golf gloves are more sensitive than others, sort of like condoms. But the golf glove serves no purpose. Unless it is cold, you might try removing it while putting.

Shoes: On real windy days you might consider long spikes if the rules on the course you play will allow it. We know of no research that indicates one type of shoe is superior to another when it comes to putting. However, as crazy as it sounds, at least one golf clinic we know of has the participants remove their shoes and go barefooted on the putting green to teach sensitivity and awareness. We don't recommend taking your shoes off, but on wet days try a water resistant golf shoe.

Peter Dobereiner (1991), the famous sports writer, mentioned in *Golf Digest* in 1986, that he unearthed a piece of research relating that the first team to climb Mount Everest discovered how much weight the expeditions could carry, and how far, and how best to carry it. A person could carry seven times as much weight on the back or shoulders as on the feet for the same degree of fatigue. Dobereiner goes on to site senior golfers, "Pensioners who have changed to light-weight shoes are tripping around golf courses like two-year olds and scoring better, for fatigue affects concentration" (p. 127). While you are at it you might as well throw in a couple of Dr. Scholl's foot pads, but keep in mind "Hogan's Law of Self-Delusions: Putting is 10 percent agony and 90 percent luck" (p.19).

Headgear: On a continuum from best (top) to worst (bottom):

> Annika Sorenstam
> Phil Mickelson
> Nancy Lopez
> Lee Trevino
> Ben Hogan
> Payne Stewart
> Sam Snead
> Greg Norman
> Chi Chi Rodriguez
> Bob Murphy
> Jim Thorpe
> Tiger Woods' mother
> Jesper Parnevik

Try a hat you feel comfortable with, one that fits and one that keeps the sun out of your eyes.

Firmness of Grip: Do not grip the club so firm that is causes muscle tension, and do not grip it so loose the club head gets wobbly. Grip the club about as firm as a baby grabs your finger to pull up or as a child holds your finger while taking his or her first steps.

Hand Placement: Try different hand placements. Experiment with all types of hand placements. The purpose of the hand placement is to give you sensitivity to the club face and control of the putter head.

Width of Stance: Just get comfortable. We suggest the feet be placed about the width of your shoulders and perpendicular to the aimline.

Distribution of Weight: Have optimum balance to form a base for the pendulum swing. Put even distribution of your weight on both feet. Unlike other sports, you neither need to get on the balls of your feet nor wear a supporter or sports bra. The distribution of your weight from toe to heal should be even. Many good golfers put a little more weight on the forward foot; 60 percent of the weight on the forward foot and 40 percent on the back.

Shoulders: To correctly master the pendulum motion, align your shoulders parallel to the aimline. As you begin your backstroke, tip your shoulders, ever so slightly, to move the putter head back. Reverse this tipping action to stroke the ball. What moves the putter head is the tipping of the shoulders, not the movement of your wrists or forearms. Your wrists and forearms stay motionless throughout the stroke.

Your shoulders form the base of an inverted triangle with your hands gripping the club being the opposing point of the triangle. The pendulum stroke is most properly executed when the triangle remains constant throughout the stroke. The apex of the tipping action is located at the back of your lower neck just above your shoulder blades.

Forearms: Forearm rotation feels natural, but it makes putting more difficult, more inconsistent, and less effective. According to Pelz (2000) forearm rotation makes it difficult to square the putter face on contact, and it supplies unwanted and unnecessary power. "Let your forearms swing back and through straight down the line, and imagine maintaining your forearm's perfect parallel-left alignment, you'll feel a perfectly natural putting stroke. And the back of your left hand and your putter face will remain square to your intended line at all times" (p. 100). Do not rotate your forearms.

Wrists: When using the pendulum motion do not cock, release, or turn your wrists. Your hands form a point of the inverted triangle with the shoulders being the base. Your wrists form the angle of the point your hands make. This wrist angle remains constant throughout the stroke.

Breathing: Sometimes when a golfer gets anxious the breathing can become constricted and shallow. While putting you want the breathing to be deep and relaxed. The key is to be aware that tension and deep breathing are incompatible. So before your subconscious makes you anxious, just consciously control your breathing. You may want to incorporate deep breathing into your pre-shot routine. The easiest way to do this is to take a deep breath as you line up the putt from behind the ball while determining the aimline. Make one good inhale and exhale before addressing the ball.

There are two things to remember to be a smart breather. First, inhale through your nose and feel the air travel down the back of your throat, past your backbone and down to your tailbone. Hold it briefly. Second, exhale through your mouth with the tip of your tongue touching the front part of the roof of your mouth where your front teeth join the rest of your mouth. After completing the exhale, walk to your ball for the address and breathe normally.

When you do this repeatedly, it will become automatic, and you will become more and more relaxed as a putter. If you feel anxious at anytime during the putt, you have probably fallen out of your breathing routine during your pre-shot routine. Remember, tension and deep breathing are incompatible, and you can control your breathing.

Pre-Shot Routine: The purpose of the pre-shot routine is to keep your subconscious mind occupied while the conscious mind surveys the situation to determine direction and distance. The conscious mind is taking in a lot of information to determine the aimline and speed while the subconscious works on tempo and rhythm. If you get out of sync, it is best to start over. According to Parent (2002), "Billy Casper, one of the all-time great champions, used to go so far as to put the club back in the bag and start over from there" (p. 89).

You can choose any procedure you want, but it must be the same every time — just like tying your shoelaces. But the routine should neither be rushed nor take too long.

It is important to get the conscious and subconscious working together and not fighting one another. During the pre-shot routine as well as while stroking the putt, you must have clarity of mind and be focused. If you catch yourself having a conversation with yourself, it is unlikely you will get the subconscious to cooperate. Anytime you consciously try to stroke the ball, the subconscious will always try to outmaneuver the conscious. It is like trying to force yourself to walk, it gets awkward.

As you approach the green, get the lay of the land. Take in as much information that is relevant to putting a good stroke on the ball. The pre-shot routine begins when you line up the ball. Try this:

1. Mark the ball, pick it up, and clean it.

2. Replace the ball with the sightline on the ball pointing straight down the aimline (See Ball section). Pick up your marker.

3. Step back two or three paces, kneel down, and double check the sightline. If it is correct proceed, if not readjust the sightline.

4. Stand up and swing the club in a pendulum motion several times while looking at the ball and cup. The practice swinging is perpendicular to the aimline with the sole purpose of judging the distance through touch, feel, and rhythm.

5. Take a smart breath (See Breathing section).

6. Step forward and address the ball.

7. Now without consciously thinking, just like walking, tying your shoelaces, and feeding your face, stroke the ball.

Using this technique maximizes the utilization of the subconscious mind to adjust and self-correct as well as help focus on putting a good stroke on the ball.

Simply stated, the routine in the beginning preoccupies the subconscious, so it doesn't get into a conversation with the conscious. The conscious takes in as much information as it can though the senses and begins to determine the direction and distance. The conscious and subconscious are working in tandem to determine direction and distance. Slowly the conscious yields its power to the subconscious. The result is you begin to trust your stroke. You actually give up control to get control. The minute you try to control the ball or control your stroke, you are in trouble.

Rhythm: Rhythm in putting refers to the flow or movement of the stroke. It is the temporal development of moving the club head back and forth. It is the regular recurrence of the various parts of the swing. Real golfers have their own personal body rhythm: some walk faster, some walk slower; some eat faster, some eat slower. Good putters capitalize on their own natural rhythm.

People who walk fast usually don't eat slow and vice versa. Capitalizing on a person's natural rhythm means they don't try to spit against the wind. They don't try to make water run up hill. They go with the flow. Real golfers who have a slow rhythm walk slow, eat slow, go through their putting routine slow, stroke the ball slow, and retrieve the ball from the cup slow.

By using the pendulum motion real golfers set their own rhythm. Once their own rhythm is established, what remains to be understood is plain physics. In a pure pendulum swing, the time it takes the very far part of the back swing to get to the very end of the follow through is the same regardless of the length of the arc.

In grandfather clocks, the timing of the swing motion remains constant. Thus, as the swing of the pendulum decays, the clock continues to keep perfect time. Real golfers don't understand this, but they accept it as fact. So when you want the ball to roll farther, you increase the length of the arc rather than try to accelerate the speed of the club head. When the rhythm remains the same, you can judge distance by the length of the back swing rather than trying to get your muscles to tell your subconscious how hard to hit the ball.

Most people agree that direction is easier to judge than distance. The reason direction is easier to determine than distance is because you can see direction, but you feel distance. Seeing is more objective than feeling. Your seeing senses are more defined and precise than the feeling senses. When using the pendulum stroke with the same rhythm, you can use both your seeing senses and your feeling senses to determine distance.

As you groove your stroke with the same rhythm, you begin to examine how far the putt travels on a level green under regular playing conditions with varying lengths of back swing. Depending on your rhythm, you will find on a six-inch back swing that the ball will roll about four to five feet; on an eight-inch back swing about six to seven feet; on a ten-inch back swing about ten to eleven feet; on a twelve-inch back swing about sixteen to seventeen feet.

Adrenaline: As pressure mounts the heart beats faster, and the body produces adrenaline, which causes the muscles to get stronger. According to Billy Balata, in his self-help golf satire, *Being the Ball*, adrenaline unleashes extra energy for your instinct of fight or flight. "It is the strength summoned by soccer Moms to lift a car off a baby" (p. 21). While putting you don't need this much strength, but inevitably adrenaline happens. There are four ways to handle adrenaline: a) artificially produce it, b) direct attention away from it, c) minimize its effect, and d) use it.

1. Artificially produce it: You can teach yourself to handle adrenaline by putting pressure on yourself through competition coupled with a wager. The amount of adrenaline produced is directly proportional to the amount of money you can't afford to lose. If you are not a betting person, you can produce adrenaline while practicing by not allowing yourself to quit until you achieve a specified goal like holing ten three-footers in a row (Pelz, 2000, p. 115).

2. Direct attention away from it: Focus your attention on the process and away from the result (Gallwey, 1998, pp. 75-

77). You can control your swing, but you can only influence the ball. Adrenaline is produced primarily when you get excited, anxious,, or scared. You get more excited, more anxious and more scared when you try to control something you can't control. When you focus on perfecting your stroke and reinforce yourself for executing a smooth-as-silk stroke with head still, contact the ball on the sweet spot, pendulum swing with good rhythm, putter head square and swing on the aimline path, you will experience less stress, less anxiety, and produce less adrenaline than if you focus on converting the putt.

3. Minimize its effect: Groove your stroke with the pendulum motion that requires no conscious thought and very little muscle movement. The simpler the stroke, the less the muscle movement, and the less the muscle movement, the less adrenaline effects the putt.

4. Use it: Use adrenaline and pressure to sharpen your focus and improve your concentration. Small amounts of adrenaline produced by excitement are healthy. By controlling your own positive excitement just prior to stroking the putt, you enhance confidence that leads to Olympian focus. You can get your juices flowing by envisioning, feeling, hearing, tasting, and smelling success before it happens. All golfers are capable of generating their own excitement on demand, but the procedures for doing so vary from player to player. Chapter 8, *PeopleWise® Putting*, explains in detail how to improve your putting by matching your natural tendency to get excited with a procedure designed to teach you how to intentionally insert excitement into your putting routine. Chapter 9, Your Brain, introduces you to an instrument that leads you to your own personalized program for enhancing your excitement which is the backbone of becoming a skilled PeopleWise® putter.

Individuals who have a tendency to fold under pressure may want to consider any one or combination of the four ways to handle adrenaline but to become a PeopleWise® putter and attain the status of being very, very good the mastering of step four is mandatory. Use it but use it intelligently.

Beyond Adrenaline: Nerves, Yips

When you allow tension to get to you, first the grip tightens, then the forearms, then shoulders. Then the body and legs stiffen, and finally the brain tightens. You now have a case of the nerves, and in extreme cases you get the jerks, jumps, twitches, explosions, and paralysis referred to as the yips. The yips are a brain spasm that impairs the putting stroke. Dr. Wolfgang Schady, consultant lecturer in neurology at Manchester University, identified the yips as occupational cramps that also affect violinists, telegraphers, and milkers (Dobereiner, 1991, p. 77). This must have aided greatly in the development of the milking machine.

Yips commonly occur when a short putt should be made. Tommy Armour devotes an entire chapter on the yips in his classic book, *Tommy Armour's ABC's of Golf*. He quotes from the great Harry Vardon's book written in 1912, *How to Play Golf*, a personal reflection that Vardon shared when he got the yips.

> This lack of confidence which overtook me when I was playing a short putt was something altogether worse than nervousness. As I stood addressing the ball, I would watch for my right hand to jump. At the end of about two seconds I would not be looking at the ball at all. My gaze would have become riveted on my right hand. I simply could not resist the desire to discover what I was going to do. Directly I felt that it was about to jump I would snatch at the ball in a desperate effort to play the shot before the involuntary movement could take effect. Up would go my head and body with a start

and off would go the ball — anywhere but on a proper line…I felt completely comfortable with putts of three yards or more and could play them satisfactorily. It was only when I got to within four feet of the hole that I became conscious of the difficulties… As a generator of confidence I would recommend a course of putting in the dark. There is a lot of imagination in seeing a line all the way from the ball to the hole. (Armour, 1967, pp. 179-180)

Armour goes on to state cigarettes, aspirin, Alka Seltzer, and whiskey are of no benefit and then quotes the great entertainer W. C. Fields: "I took a cup of booze to quiet my nerves. I repeated the treatment until my nerves got so quiet I couldn't move" (p. 109).

When a desperate player seeks advice on what to do when suffering from nerves or worse, the yips, many writers, including Armour, tell them to do "nothing." This response of "nothing" is a little tongue-in-cheek humor yet sprinkled with a bit of wisdom, because what they are implying is the nervousness and yips are in your head. As everyone knows, it has nothing to do with physical incapacity or lack of knowledge. It is all psychological.

The simplest solution is to clear it out of your head by not thinking at all. However, your mind is a workaholic. It works day and night, when you are awake and asleep. The bottom line is, your mind has fixed in on what *could* happen instead of what *should* happen.

There are many temporary solutions to nerves and yips but the only permanent solution is to take control of your own subconscious by programming your brain into seeing and feeling success before you execute the stroke. As mentioned earlier this is the foundation of PeopleWise® Putting and is explained in detail in Chapter 8. Also, refer to the previous section on Adrenaline.

If you ever get the case of the yips, it may be comforting to know the great Bernhard Langer as a teenager had the worst case of the yips. He used to rejoice on rare occasions when he did not have a four-putt green in his round. He later became ranked at the top of the European Tour's putting statistics (Dobereiner, 1991, p. 78).

Reading the Greens: There isn't really much to be said that will be of any value to the weekend golfer about reading the greens. Weekend golfers know the greens better than a topographer, horticulturist, surveyor and civil engineer combined. Once the real golfer stalks the putt with their wisdom and seasoned eye, they know without delay the direction and speed needed to convert the putt. They don't need a caddie or a greens consultant.

There are two pointers that every real golfer knows but needs to be reminded of from time to time:

1. The majority of short putts are missed by looking for imaginary slopes and hitting the ball softly, trying to "baby" it in the cup. *Stroke short putts firmly if not boldly.* Peter Dobereiner, in his book *Golf a la Carte*, tells the story of Little Mac, who caddied for Dai Rees. Little Mac would size up a putt for Rees by looking through opera glasses from which the lenses had long since vanished, then advise, "Hit is slightly straight sir" (p. 31).

2. Putts that are going to move to the right or left are missed on the low side. Pelz (2000) indicates, "90 percent of the misses are below the hole" (p. 158). This is why the low side is referred to as the "amateur side." *Fudge on the high side.*

Studying the grain is the means used to determine the direction in which the blades of grass grow. The ball, depending on the speed, will move ever so slightly, if at all, with the grain. Grain can be affected by sunlight, wind, or water surface.

To read the grain, crouch down with the sun at your back, and look at the grass across the green. If you see a sheen to it, the grain is leaning away from you. If the grass looks dull, you are against the grain. Balls supposedly roll more slowly against the grain and faster with the grain. If the grass between the ball and the hole is leaning left, the ball will have a tendency to move left. If it is leaning right, the ball will move right.

Bermuda grass has broad bristly leaves and sparse growing patterns and can be somewhat grainy. Bent grass has some grain, but it isn't too strong.

At the risk of stating the obvious, downhill putts roll faster than uphill putts. Longer blades of grass slow the ball down while shorter grass speeds up the putt. Wet greens are slower than dry greens, and short dry burned out greens are real fast.

Green speed is determined with a Stimpmeter. A slow green is a seven, where the ball rolls seven feet from a given height on the Stimpmeter. "A ten is fast, most PGA tournaments shoot for a 10.5 to 11. Green roll at 12 to 13 are very fast and sometimes referred to as Augusta fast because that is the speed at Augusta National Golf Club, home of The Masters every spring" (Pelz, 2000, p. 62).

The plumb-bob is based on the principle of a plumb line which has a weight attached to the end of a string that hangs straight down from the force of gravity resulting in the line being exactly vertical or plumbed. This allows builders to erect tall buildings that are straight up and down and won't topple over regardless of the levelness of the ground.

Hold the putter at arms length in front of you, with the thumb and forefinger securing the top of the grip with the shaft hanging straight down. To assure the putter shaft is straight down turn the toe of the putter directly away from your body. Placing the club head perpendicular to your body helps gravity guide the shaft straight down from your eye view.

Once the shaft is as vertical as you can get it, crouch down a little and look at the contours of the green using the plumbed shaft as a reference point. Truthfully, most real golfers can sense which way the green slopes without any device whatsoever. Plumb-bobbing does look good though in the hands of a focused weekend golfer, especially when they close one eye. At this juncture it may be wise to mention Mahaffey's Moan: "Even if you read the break, the grain will get you" (Dobereiner, 1991, p. 19).

Touch and Feel: To the real golfer touch and feel are somewhat synonymous. Technically, touch is what you do to the ball and feel is what the ball does to you. Pelz (2000) identifies touch as knowing *what* to do primarily when determining distance. Feel is knowing *how* to do it, as the process relates to sensitivity, awareness, and kinesthetic movement.

Touch is learned; feel is experienced. Touch is more objectively learned based on seeing where the ball ends up after multiple trials. Touch is determining how hard to hit the ball.

Feel is having a sense of rhythm and an appreciation for the delicacy of the shot. Feel is subjectively learned through experience.

Comparing and contrasting both touch and feel or determining the similarities and differences may best be left to psychologists and academicians because to the real golfer the important thing is to know the direction and distance then determine how to get it there.

To become a PeopleWise® putter, to achieve real, real good status regardless of your personality or how and where the activation of your brain takes place, you must develop touch and learn to feel success prior to the execution of the task. This is referred to throughout this book and is the foundation for becoming a PeopleWise® putter. For developing touch and feel pay particular attention to the following:

Chapter 3, Nuts and Bolts, sections Head Still, Sweet Spot and Smooth Stroke.

Head Still: See Gallwey's inner golf awareness technique.

Sweet Spot: The entire section incorporates feel.

Smooth Stroke: Review the very last part that deals with distance.

Chapter 4, Too Much, Pre-Shot Routine and Rhythm sections.

Pre-Shot Routine: See Step 4.

Rhythm: Pay particular attention to the part on determining distance.

Chapter 6, Mind Control, Steps 5 and 6.

Step 5, Engage in self-talk: Focus attention on the emotion.
Step 6, Do this ten seconds at a time, three times a day:
Study the relationship of POWs to emotion.

Chapter 8, PeopleWise® Putting, the section Forebrain, Level 6, Sociocentric.

Forebrain Dominant: Although each dominant area of the brain utilizes feeling, the Forebrain explanations spotlight feelings and sensitivity.

Chapter 9, Your Brain, PeopleWise® Pattern Descriptions Level 6, Level 5-6, and Level 4-6.

Level 6, Sociocentric: Shows the importance of feeling
in a pure sense.
Level 5-6, Materialist-Sociocentric Blend: Illustrates the power
of feeling using right and forebrain.
Level 4-6, Absolutist-Sociocentric Blend: Illustrates the power
of feeling using the left and forebrain.

Everything in this chapter is trimming; it is at times useful but not essential in every case. Chapter 3, Nuts and Bolts, gave you the essentials related to mechanics. The remaining Chapters 5, Eighty Percent; 6, Mind Control; 7, Brain Science; 8, PeopleWise® Putting; and 9, Your Brain, are the essentials related to the mental part of putting.

CHAPTER 5
Eighty Percent

When you are, without consciously thinking, able to keep your head still, hit the ball on the sweet spot, and master a pendulum motion by keeping the putter head square to the aimline while swinging on the aimline path, you will be a good putter. You will be able to putt on a level green at the average of what a professional, on-tour golfer, putts on undulating green. Now, to be a *real* good putter you must master the mental part. Miller (1996) quotes the legendary Ben Hogan as saying, "Golf is twenty percent technique and eighty percent mental" (p. 106).

What separates the professional golfer on tour from all those other excellent want-to-be golfers trying to get on tour is mental savvy. Furthermore, for those on tour, what separates the great from the good, a legend from a top professional, the champion from the runner-up is mental toughness. At this level, superior performance doesn't have anything to do with better physical attributes or better mechanical execution. Superior performance relies on a superior mental attitude.

To realize the value of one millisecond ask the person who has won a *silver* medal in the Olympics. As one approaches world class, we may be talking millimeters and nanoseconds. For the weekend golfer, we are striving for a personal best.

To get real good you must be confident. You must believe the ball is going into the hole. "Ben Crenshaw, one of the all-time great putters, said that when he was really putting well he could smell the dirt in the bottom of the hole" (Parent, 2002, p.41). What is confidence? Confidence is smelling the dirt in the bottom of the hole. It is knowing you are going to be successful before you execute the task. Confidence is knowing the ball is going into the hole before it is struck.

Confidence can be developed, taught, and harnessed. Confidence can and will overshadow doubt. Confidence is mastering mind control. Mind control is the next skill you will master to become a real good putter.

The foundation for understanding how to control your mind comes from the seminal works of three great motivational experts: Maxwell Maltz, author of *Psycho-Cybernetics*, Dennis Waitley, author of *Seeds of Greatness* and Louis Tice, author of *A Better World, A Better You*. These best selling masterpieces, written by these three scholars have not only popularized the mental aspects of performance, they have operationalized it so it can be learned and taught. In golfing circles, the mental part is often referred to as visual imagery and mental rehearsal.

The understanding of the mental aspects of performance is simple but mastering it takes great discipline. Notice, it takes discipline not practice. This chapter is the key to becoming real good.

Understanding the comfort zone: First we must understand the comfort zone.

Flippa Rose is a fictional weekend golfer with whom we can identify. Instead of playing on the weekend, she plays every Wednesday because that is the day designated for women at the Sunshine Country Club. Flippa is one of the better golfers in her group and carries a ten handicap. This morning she is on a roll. She finished the front nine one over and she parred 10 through 15. She bogeyed 16 but birdied 17. On 18 she lands on the green in regulation, and if she two putts she will score a 73, the best she has ever scored.

You would think she would be excited and eager to putt, but she is nervous and fidgety. Her forehead beads with sweat, and her heart is pounding with an unusual thumpety-thump. She sizes up her putt, goes through her pre-shot routine remembering to take a deep breath, but somehow her hands shake, and the club head gets wobbly. So she grips the club more firmly. Because of the firmness of her grip, she develops tension in her shoulders. She just wants to get it into "gimmie" range for a personal best.

She knows she isn't ready, and she should step back to get some composure, but she can't wait. She wants to get it over with. Before she knows what is happening, she jerks her putter forward and strikes the ball way too hard. The ball shoots forward then suddenly begins to track toward the hole. Before her very eyes, the ball strikes the back of the cup and drops out of sight. Stunned, she can't believe it, less than one percent of the golfers in America have scored par or better. Her partner jumps up and down charges toward her to give a big hug, while her opponents smile in disbelief uttering, "Great shot." A spirit of celebration resounds in the air and when the golf pro finds out what happened, he issues a free round of drinks to the entire group. Her signed score card is proudly pinned on the bulletin board next to the water cooler for all to see.

Now think what has happened. Flippa has demonstrated she can shoot par, a 72. She has done it, experienced it, and been reinforced for it. Anyone would think she would do it again, but you know, we know and the world knows that during the next round she will not shoot a 72. She won't even shoot her average, 82. She will most likely score significantly above her average in the low to middle 90s. Why? She pictures herself as an 82, and when she scores around 82, she feels comfortable. Sometimes she will score a little lower and sometimes a little higher, but her average stays around 82 no matter how much she practices. All of a sudden she scores par, ten below her handicap. She is excited, happy, even ecstatic, but she is uncomfortable. She has performed outside her comfort zone. A 72 is not normal. A 72 is beyond her grasp, beyond her highest expectation. Simply put, the 72 was just plain old luck. It just sort of happened. It came out of left field. So the very next time she will score in the 90s and then she will say, "I knew it, I'm an 82er, I'm a ten handicapper." Then she will settle back, relax and get her feet firmly planted in her ten handicap comfort zone.

Everyone has seen this happen or has experienced it, yet no one understands this phenomenon. The answer is, the comfort zone knows math, and it can add, subtract, multiply, and divide. The comfort zone is what makes us sane, what makes us real, what makes us "us." If Flippa continued to score par, she would not know how to act. She would go out of her mind because she knows deep down inside that par is not her. She is not in the one percent of golfers in this land, she is an 82er.

As reported by Gallwey (1998),

> At a recent conference of the PGA of America on teaching and coaching, *Golf Tips* magazine pointed out that "a question that arose repeatedly was this: Why is it that, despite the proliferation of golf schools, talented instructors, training aids, reputable instruction books and magazines as well as high-tech, game-improving equipment, the handicap of the average American golfer is at best stagnant and — more likely — on the rise, according to United States Golf Studies." (p. xvi)

The bad news is, scores are not improving. The major reason is because the weekend golfer has been psychologically strangled by a self-imposed comfort zone. The good news is, we can outsmart the comfort zone.

1-800-514-7626 • P.O. Box 215 • University, MS 38677
mm@watervalley.net
www.managementandmotivation.com

JAMES S. PAYNE
President

MANAGEMENT & MOTIVATION, INC.

ıfort zone: Second, we must outsmart, ɔmfort zone.

ɛeding week, after shooting par, delusions of going on tour. Each ɩarily dreams about her accom- ɪewly acquired skill. No, at this d skill. It is a gift. The following ɑrrives at Sunshine Country Club ɩ. She hits a bucket of balls and ing stroke on the practice green.

ɛ, join her, and engage in the ɪt Flippa isn't listening. She is ɪɩɪɪɪkɪɪg, ɔjecting, what she is going to do today.

On the first hole there is a row of hedges lined down the right side of the fairway and marking the out of bounds. Flippa addresses the ball, glances at the middle of the fairway where she wants to place the ball, but in her peripheral vision she catches the sight of the hedges on the right. For some reason the hedges seem to have grown a little from last week and are leaning left. Flippa is focused, even more focused, more determined than in previous rounds because she plans to shoot *sub par* today.

In a fleeting moment, in just a flick of an eye she thinks, "Let's get started real good. Keep it left. Don't go into the hedges. Don't go out of bounds."

The scenario ends here because we all know she will hit not one but two balls out of bounds, and at the end of the day she will post a disgusting 93, her worst score since winter. While spraying the ball all over the course, she at first gets upset, then disappointed, no, down right spitting mad. As reality sets in and her fantasy of tour play fades, an air of serenity slowly diffuses her psychic space because mathematically she is entering her comfort zone. As she settles into her comfort zone reality sinks in that a ten handicap is good. It is something to be proud of. After all she is one of the top players in the club. She relaxes now in the comfort of her own zone.

Don't underestimate the power of the comfort zone. How many times have we finished the front nine, surprisingly way below our established handicap, only to shoot a terrible back nine to average it out. Or the reverse, hit a terrible front nine only to score a brilliant back nine to average it out. When we find ourselves functioning outside our comfort zone, things happen to put us smack dab back into the middle of our comfort zone. That is what makes us who we are.

Flippa has the talent and the game to shoot 72, but simply put, her comfort zone won't let her. In fact, the comfort zone won't even let her get her handicap in the single digits. She is imprisoned by her own mind. Not only did her poor performance validate her picture of being a ten handicapper, it confirmed her companions' hunch that last week she was just lucky. Let's face it. Flippa Rose is a ten handicapper.

Some people believe they can't remember names. They are of normal intelligence, and their minds work perfectly, but no matter how much they try, how much they practice, how many memory courses they take, if they believe they can't remember names, then they just flat won't remember names. The comfort zone is so very powerful it locks us into acting and behaving as we see ourselves and believe ourselves to be. We act and behave in accordance with our picture. Our picture is our life's target. Our comfort zone is nothing more than a target of life. What keeps us on target, what keeps us functioning within our comfort zone is the creative subconscious.

Maxwell Maltz, M.D., a famous plastic surgeon and bestselling author of *Psycho-Cybernetics*, suggests the mind (creative subconscious) is like a homing system in a torpedo or an automatic pilot.

Once the target is set, the self-adjusting mechanism guides the missile toward the target through a monitoring feedback system. This navigational guidance system constantly adjusts the flight of the missile by keeping it on target. Just as the propulsion of the missile drives it forward, the creative subconscious drives our behavior and actions. In other words, the creative subconscious is our motivator. The creative subconscious motivates us to perform within our comfort zone.

We cannot control the creative subconscious. The creative subconscious is always programmed to guide our behaviors and actions toward our picture, toward our comfort zone, toward our target. But the beauty is we can move our picture, change our comfort zone, select a new target. We can outsmart our comfort zone by talking ourselves into believing we are different. We can tell ourselves over and over again, with such conviction, that we can actually see a new picture of ourselves, vividly, in high resolution. As we construct a new target of ourselves, the creative subconscious will drive us, monitor us, to become it.

It is easy to outsmart the comfort zone because it believes what it hears and feels. Flippa Rose had the skill, talent, and game to be a par shooter. What she didn't have was the confidence or belief she could do it. Her picture of being a ten handicapper got in her way. To work the mental part of her game she could have begun to imagine herself shooting par. She could tell herself, "I like myself as I shoot par, I see myself shooting par. I see people watching me with admiration and some with envy. I see them studying my form and rhythm. I hear them jumping with joy when I sink putts. I feel the exuberance in the air as I pump my fist after a stellar shot. I feel the happiness in my heart as I strut down the fairway. I feel the wind blow through my hair as I walk with pride. I see my name at the top of the leader board. I am in the one percent of golfers in this universe. I am *par* and I love it."

By talking to herself in this manner, she could begin to alter her picture of herself moving from a ten handicapper to a par shooter. She could change her comfort zone, her target. Now, with her new picture, as she prepares for her match she gains confidence because she sees herself in a new light. She sees herself successfully shooting par. She will find that she has greater focus and improved concentration.

You have the power to change your target, but you cannot change or control the creative subconscious. The creative subconscious is nothing more than a homing device that drives your behaviors and actions toward the target.

Outsmarting the comfort zone is nothing more than forcing ourselves to see our new picture, our new target. Fortunately, through the works of Maxwell Maltz, Dennis Waitley, Louis Tice and others, we have a program that helps us force ourselves to see ourselves in a different light. As we force ourselves to see it, we develop Mind Control.

CHAPTER 6
Mind Control

There are nine basic steps to mastering mind control, or as they say in golfing circles, visual imagery and mental rehearsal. When you master these, you will elevate yourself to the status of being a *real* good putter.

1. Get a picture of what you want, not what you don't want.

This sounds simple, but you will find it isn't as simple as it appears. Many times we focus on what we don't want rather than what we want. We think about not slicing the golf ball as opposed to imagining where we want to hit it, right in the middle of the fairway. Some golfers hit the ball well all day until they come to a hole where they have to hit it over a body of water. They become blinded by the water. They can't see over it, so they take out a water ball, an old, beat-up thing. What does this tell the subconscious? What does this have to do with confidence? The focus is on not hitting it in the water instead of focusing on where the ball is to land.

Many times we focus on not embarrassing ourselves instead of seeing ourselves performing perfectly. We focus on the fact that we don't want to fail instead of identifying success patterns. It is easy and for some people very natural, to focus on what they don't want rather than what they want.

Louis Tice, renowned motivational expert, refers to this as the "Rock in the Road." He tells the story of learning how to ride a bike. As we begin, it is hard to keep our balance. Soon, we find it easier to keep the bike balanced if the bike is moving forward; however, because we are unsteady and somewhat unstable, we often find ourselves heading in directions we don't want to go. Many beginning riders find themselves moving forward only to spot a rock in the road. The more we try to steer away from the rock, the more the rock pulls us toward it. Rather than looking at where we want to go, we look at where we don't want to go — we can't take our eyes off the rock. Tice advises, "Don't lead your people to the rock in the road and don't lead yourself to the rock in the road."

2. Clarify your desire in terms of effort, time, money, risk.

Bringing about a change in your picture will cost you something. You must be willing to pay the price. Mind control costs. Mind control will take some effort, yet you can't force it. It takes effort and energy. Although initially it won't take a lot of time, later, you might get addicted to the process and find you are utilizing mind control techniques many times throughout the day on important things in your life outside of golf. The monetary cost is usually minimal; however, sometimes aids and self-help devices such as background sound tapes or specific personal development books will be helpful. The real price comes in your willingness to take a risk. You must conquer the fear of failure that so often accompanies risk. One of the best ways to handle fear is to determine what is the worst thing that could happen. In most cases, it isn't severe. We are not talking life or death here. We are talking about putting. Keep a sense of humor and work at mind control intently, but don't take it too seriously.

3. Maintain perspective.

As you make the effort and pay the price, it is important to be sure that what you chart out to do is healthy and beneficial. Make sure it is the right thing to do and it makes you a better person. The key lies in perspective. Your target is to get the putt to fall in the hole, or if you choose not to be so result oriented, the target is to put a stellar stroke on the ball.

Because there are so many things you can't control that affect a putt, a strong case can be made to form a picture only of your stroke since you can control all aspects of the stroke. Some very good putters take pride in their stroke, and when the ball doesn't fall they praise themselves for stroking the ball perfectly and blame the grass or green for keeping the ball out of the cup. Most certainly, focusing on the process of putting is far less fear provoking and less doubt inflicting than focusing on results of getting the ball in the hole.

Whether you focus on the process or the result, to make visual imagery and mental rehearsal work, your picture must be very clear. Keep in mind, most of the time it takes two putts to get the ball in the hole, so roughly you fail 50 percent of the time if you are result oriented. The real character builder is how you react physically and mentally when you miss a putt that is six feet or less from the hole. The shorter the putt, the higher the expectation. The higher the expectation, when you miss, the greater the disappointment. Parent (2002) makes an important point, "the hopes and fears that create mental obstacles intensify as we get closer to our objective; the ball going into the hole" (p. xix). He goes on to say, "Be 100 percent optimistic about and committed to your shot before you make it, and then 100 percent realistic (and forgiving and kind to yourself) about the results" (p. 49).

> As my daughter Kim became more skillful, I noticed she became more emotional when she didn't play well. I would try to console her and explain it was only a game, but this didn't seem to help much.
>
> I developed an insight regarding the over reaction to play when I became a certified facilitator for conducting seminars on *The Seven Habits of Highly Effective People.* Stephen Covey, master teacher and famous author of the seven habits explained what he did when his son would over-react after losing in a soccer match. He laid out five goals by asking these questions:

1. Did you win?
2. Did you try your hardest?
3. Were you a team player?
4. Did you learn anything?
5. Did you have fun?

These five goals will put things in perspective for anyone who is singularly focused on winning. I adapted these goals to golf with Kim. Our five goals were expressed in these questions:

1. Did you win?
2. Did you try?
3. Were you a lady?
4. Did you learn?
5. Did you have fun?

She admitted she had more fun when she won but she got the picture. She began to put more perspective in her picture as a player.

Sprinkling a lot of perspective in your picture gives it depth and substance.

4. Imagine the end result in vivid detail.

Once you get a picture of what you want, are willing to pay the price for it, and have decided that is the right thing, then it is important to begin to perfect the image in the most vivid detail possible. The clarity of this picture in the highest resolution is the foundation for real mind control. Here visual imagery and mental rehearsal become real.

You must create this picture in such a way that you can see it, hear it, feel it, smell it, and taste it. The clearer and more focused the target, the more efficiently the tracking device of the creative subconscious will work. What motivates a person is not the picture; what motivates the person is the creative subconscious. If the picture is vague, the tracking device doesn't know exactly where to go, so it vacillates all over the place. When the picture is pin-pointed, the tracking device is razor sharp.

Even though the subconscious mind cannot distinguish between an imagined picture from the real thing, the subconscious mind also cannot create a clearer, more vivid picture. Only the conscious mind can craft a vivid image in high resolution. You must now begin to work the conscious part of your mind, realizing your conscious mind has been programmed over time to cope and survive rather than construct and create.

Parent (2002) sums it up with, "the image is the message our body responds to and does its best to produce" (p. 44). "When you tune in the vividness of the moment, your body gets clear instruction on where you intend to go, and your thoughts don't interfere with how you get there" (p. 42).

Don't confuse concern about the result with envisioning the result. "Concern about the result is different from envisioning a result you intend" (p. 92).

Once we get a picture of what we want without leading ourselves to the rock in the road, and we are willing to pay the price, and we choose to do what will make us better, and we get the picture in our head clearly focused in high resolution, then we are ready to talk ourselves into taking action.

5. Engage in self-talk: talk, picture, emotion.

Dennis Waitley, former Olympic motivational coach, operationalized mind control by perfecting self-talk. Self-talk takes on four dimensions: (a) first person, (b) present tense, (c) positive, and (d) action-emotion oriented. In other words, he perfected visual imagery and mental rehearsal.

- First person: Start with "I." I like to putt because I am good. I putt with intensity and focus.

- Present tense: State it as of "now." Even though Flippa was a ten handicapper she must see herself as a par shooter and a proud member of the one percent golfers in America *now at this time.*

- Positive: Put a positive spin on it, and don't lead yourself to the rock in the road. I see myself as a good putter, not I don't want to three putt. Stay away from negative thoughts such as, "I hate myself when my putting goes sour."

- Action-emotion oriented: Generate excitement and feeling. I feel exuberant as I sink putts right and left. I see people admiring me every time I putt and it makes me feel wonderful. I feel on top of the world when I walk on the green. I feel people envious yet so respectful as I address the putt.

The idea is to use self-talk to motivate you so that you are telling yourself what to do or to be. The more emotional you can be and the more you can feel it, the more vivid the picture becomes. Self-talk enhances the development of the image or picture you are crafting.

6. Do this ten seconds at a time, three times a day.

Engage in self-talk once in the morning, once at noon, and again before you go to bed. You must be convincing, and you must do it religiously. Rather than focus on length of time, you emphasize the number of times and intensity. The lesson of frequency has been taught through brainwashing techniques used throughout history, as revealed by prisoners of war.

As explained in the first book of the PeopleWise® series, *PeopleWise® Brain to Brain*, accounts of individuals being held captive have been recorded throughout time, but the most noted are those reported by Viktor Frankl, Captain Gerald Coffee, and Major William E. Mayer. Although many lessons are learned from POWs, the single most important lesson is how much internal strength many individuals have under seemingly dire conditions and hopeless circumstances. The importance of perseverance and the will to continue living is striking and inspirational. The flip side of this internal strength is equally as fascinating and educational.

Major William E. Mayer, a psychiatrist, conducted an exhaustive study of returning prisoners of war captured in Korea by the Chinese. The psychological methods used were deceptively simple, yet powerful and effective. Major Mayer referred to this brainwashing technique as a weapon, one as powerful as a nuclear device. The fact was up to four thousand Americans who survived those years of captivity in twelve separate camps were guarded often by as few as one armed guard per one hundred prisoners. Never, not once in the course of the entire Korean conflict, did a single American successfully, permanently escape from any established POW camp. This has never before or after happened in the history of America. No machine gun towers, no guard dogs, no electric fences, no search lights...Yet, nobody tried to escape because they were actually imprisoned by their own minds.

When the tired, scared prisoner entered the camp, rather than being beaten, tortured, or interrogated, they were extended a hand of friendship and welcomed by an individual who spoke their language, and they were asked only to keep an open mind, listen, and not to try to resist. From that point on, the prisoners went through an intense educational regime that required listening to long lectures on topics like history, civics, politics, and economics. Following the lecture, all they were required to do was to participate in discussion groups. They didn't have to agree with the teacher's point of view, they just had to participate; however, if they did agree, they were favorably recognized. The educational process was systematic, consistent, and continuous. As time went by, the prisoners were encouraged to write and give presentations supporting the teachers' viewpoints, even if they didn't believe it. It was reported by Major Mayer that many of the prisoners saw this as a joke or sham, but did, in fact, write papers and give oral presentations, taking positions against their own personal beliefs. Over time they talked themselves into acquiescing and gave up their will to try to escape. Shockingly, some gave up their will to live. Thirty-eight percent of those captured died, the highest death rate of Americans in any kind of captivity in any prison in any way since the American Revolution. They did not die because of mass execution or systematic starvation, but primarily, many just gave up. This type of death was termed "give-up-itis." These individuals would crawl into a corner, pull a blanket over their heads, and die within hours. Not starved to death. No physical disease present. They were not psychotic. They were not insane. They knew what they were doing. They made the most profound of all human surrenders. They talked themselves into giving up to the point of death.

Obviously there were many factors involved other than just talking themselves into acquiescence, such as fear, loneliness, removal of the discontents to other camps, control of the mail, etc. However, the point must be made that many of those who died and those who continued to live actually participated, believing they were lying to themselves in order to fool the enemy, but, as we have learned, the subconscious cannot distinguish fact from fiction. The subconscious has no value mechanism; it just does what it is told.

As we master our own mind control, we must keep in mind we are not prisoners of war. Therefore, we must force ourselves to continuously tell ourselves, through self-talk again and again because, over time, we will in fact, do what we tell ourselves to do. Since we are not prisoners of war, it is simple to quit. It is easy to give up because no one is making us do anything. But the minute we stop imagining and the minute we stop our self-talk, we give up controlling our mind and begin to react to the environment. When the environment controls our minds rather than us controlling our own minds, we are out of control. Mastering mind control is not easy; it is simple, but it is not easy.

7. Apply attitude, knowledge, skills.

We do not want to create a false sense of hope. Although mind control is mental and predominately attitudinal, we need to remind ourselves that in the real world, we have knowledge and skills. I can tell myself I am a good putter, but if I don't know anything about putting then all the talk and envisioning is worthless. Here is where the two rivers, mechanics and mental, must join and become one. It has been said that attitude makes up 65 percent of our success and knowledge, and skills make up the other 35 percent. Once the mechanics are mastered, it might be 20 percent mechanics and 80 percent mental, but it doesn't make any difference what the percentages are as long as we realize knowledge and skill are necessary. Without knowledge and skill we become PMA Freaks (Positive Mental Attitude Freaks). No matter how much we try we can't "think" the ball in the hole. It must be stroked.

8. When you fail, you flush first, then if necessary, you change your goal on the run.

If we do not occasionally fail, then probably we are not pushing ourselves hard enough. The ultimate challenge when using mind control is to determine our limits. However, when we do fail, we want to get back on track as soon as possible. Everyone has experienced a slump or a streak of bad luck. Why is it that if we fail once, we usually fail repeatedly? One of the major reasons is because it is so hard to get back on track. Once we fail, it is hard to get the failure out of our head. We mentally see the failure clearer than we envision success; we lead ourselves to the rock in the road. The first step to getting back on track is to flush the failure out of our mind by using a self-talk reprimand. Immediately after we fail, we tell ourselves, "That's not like me. That's not the putter I am." Then we follow this personal self-talk reprimand with positive self-talk directing us toward our picture, "head still, sweet spot, back-forward."

In *PeopleWise® Brain to Brain* this is illustrated with a story about Reggie Jackson and a personal testimonial after taking Louis Tice's training.

> It is the World Series, Yankees vs. Dodgers, 1978. Ninth inning, two out, two on. The count is three-and-two. The batter is Reggie Jackson; the pitcher is a rookie, Bob Welch. Tension mounts as millions watch on T.V. Reggie Jackson, named Mr. October because he always performed under pressure, especially in October during the World Series, fouls off one, two three balls, then suddenly strikes out. The Yankees lose, but what everyone remembers is Reggie threw a God-awful temper tantrum. He pounded the bat to the ground, raised his fists in the air, ranted, raved, cursed, yelled, stomped, and to many, made an ass of himself. Those who knew him, however, knew he was flushing that failure out of his mind and shortly thereafter he would begin to mentally prepare himself for next time.
>
> The next time Jackson faced Bob Welch, no contest — homerun, followed by two more off different pitchers.
>
> Let's imagine for a moment what it must be like to play with a person of Reggie Jackson's caliber. Think for a moment what must happen every time he strikes out — a swinging strike. He stomps back to the dugout, jams the bat into the rack, sits down on the bench, curses at himself, and fumes for a few seconds. If you were stupid enough to go over and try to console him by patting him on the back and saying "That is O.K. Reggie you'll get it next time," he would push you away, scowl at you and

shout, "Get out of my face, don't lead me to failure." Within time, he gets composure. He focuses on the pitcher. You see the intensity in his eyes. His forearms are on his knees, thumbs pressed against his forefingers, and he is imagining ball down — bat around — ball explode; ball down — bat around — ball explode; ball down — bat around — ball explode....He is mentally preparing himself for success after he has flushed failure out of his mind. By the time he gets up to bat again, he has successfully, mentally hit more than 100 pitches. Reggie Jackson, Mr. October, is a master of mind control. Reggie Jackson hit five actual homeruns in one World Series and heaven only knows how many mental ones.

Twenty years ago I took Louis Tice's New Age Thinking course. As I completed the course, I realized one thing that constantly, continuously made me angry was that I couldn't keep track of my car keys. I'd lose my car keys all the time. Every time I misplaced the keys, I'd accuse someone of moving them and when I finally would find them, I'd tell myself I could just never remember my keys. Through the work of Tice's program, I realized I was leading myself to failure. I pictured myself not being able to remember my keys. I'd self-talk myself into not remembering my keys. I believed I couldn't remember my keys. Thus I couldn't find my keys. Then, I realized, I'm of normal intelligence, my mind is normal, I have a decent memory, so I made up my mind to remember my keys. When I shut off the car, I would immediately remove the keys and put them on my belt and I would say to myself, "Keys on belt, keys on belt, keys on belt...." The first time I misplaced my keys, when I found them, I scolded myself, "That's not like me, that's not the Jim Payne I know, I'm of normal intelligence, I can remember things." Then I grabbed the keys, thrust them on my belt and said, "keys on belt, keys on belt, keys on belt." Do you realize, prior to Tice's course, I misplaced my keys all the time and after the course, I've only misplaced the keys twice, at which time I flushed the mishap out of my mind and programmed myself for success. Twenty years later, I continue to remember where my keys are. I always have my keys on my belt when I'm not driving and I'm proud of it. It makes me feel good about myself as I confidently retrieve my keys from my belt. I like myself better. I have a better self-image of myself. I never misplace my keys, never. Now, sometimes I don't know where my car is, but I always can find my keys. (pp. 31-32)

Let's say you are working on something, and you continue to fail. The rule of thumb is if you continue to fail seven to ten days or seven to ten trials, you should do something different because your mind won't let you continue to tell yourself something that isn't true. Remember, you are not a prisoner of war. No one is forcing you to continue, so you will stop your self-talk. Before stopping your self-talk, change your goal on the run. Move the goal closer.

It is unlikely that Flippa Rose will shoot par within the next seven to ten rounds, so she changes her goal on the run by saying, "I see myself as a single digit handicapper. I love shooting in the single digits, etc. etc."

You get the idea.

9. Measure the outcome — feedback.

The last step is nothing more than a feedback or monitoring process that helps us keep on track. When possible, it is helpful if we can measure our progress objectively. This can be done in numbers or percentages. Most skill development can be measured as to accuracy, amount, length, speed, etc. Sometimes a vivid clear picture is selected that can't be measured objectively, so subjective judgment comes into play.

An example where judgment could be considered is putting a smooth stroke on the ball. One must determine what a smooth stroke is and recognize it when it happens. However, even though it is subjective, it should be actually tabulated. For instance, on the scorecard, under your regular scores for each hole, you would mark the number of actual putts attempted and, in your opinion, the number of smooth strokes you made. Using this system you could calculate the percentage of smooth strokes, per attempts, per round. This database will give you a feedback loop on how well you are doing. This smooth stroke percentage could also be determined on the practice green. Even though you may not practice much, every time you do practice it will be of great assistance to count those things you are trying to picture. If you want, you can break the stroke down into sub-units and figure the percent of time the club head was square on impact, the percent of time your head kept still, etc.

The number one reason practice doesn't help improve one's game is because most people practice without a feedback system. When you practice with a feedback system, you will get better results in less time than when you practice a lot with no feedback system. In fact, when practicing without a feedback system, you are likely to get worse. Remember, what gets counted usually gets done. That which is pictured and gets done and counted, is repeated. So be sure what you picture and count is the right thing.

Flippa Rose automatically tabulates her score after each round. Now, using mind control she pictures herself a single-digit handicapper and every time she scores in the single digits she validates her picture. Thus the creative subconscious drives her toward single digits rather than mathematically shackling her to a ten handicap. It sounds so simple, yet it is so difficult to do. It is difficult to convince yourself to be something you are not, even though you could be.

To help my daughter, Kim, become a better all-around player we would take her scorecard after each round and on the scorecard actually tabulate the results of the five goals: Win, Try, Lady, Learn and Fun.

One interesting side note was one time she decided on her own to force herself to play like a lady. Sometimes, especially when missing a putt she felt she should have made, she would emit a vocal outburst. She decided to actually count every vocal outburst by marking it on the scorecard on the hole it occurred. Within a short period of time she brought her emotion under control. Here is one case where counting what you don't want actually worked. She taught herself that a missed shot didn't cause her to get angry, but she had allowed a missed shot to make her angry. By controlling her temper through picturing herself as a lady and counting un-ladylike conduct, she became a better player if not a better golfer.

So here is where we are. By mastering the mechanics without consciously thinking — head still, sweet spot, pendulum swing on the aimline — you have attained the good putter status. What remains is mental. Now when you master the nine steps of mind control, you become a real good putter. What is a real good putter? A real good putter beats the pros by five percent. Here are the figures:

Distance Feet	Good Percent	Real Good Percent
1	100	100
2	100	100
3	85	90
4	70	75
5	60	65
6	50	55
7	40	45
8	35	40
9	25	30
10	20	25

This is well within your grasp because you have the ability and intelligence coupled with a sound, repeatable stroke mastered with all that has been written, taught, and researched about the mental part of putting. You are making both rivers work for you.

If you see yourself as a poor putter, then no matter what you read or how much you practice, you will putt poorly.

If you see yourself as a good putter, you *convincingly* see yourself as a good putter and you master the mechanics of putting without consciously thinking, you will not only putt good you will putt real good.

Now, you want to get *real, real* good? Then read the rest of this book because what you are about to be exposed to has never been written before. What remains is the secret of how to control the activation of your own brain. It ain't rocket science; it's brain science.

CHAPTER 7
Brain Science

Brain science introduces ideas/concepts related to the firing of the brain, sometimes referred to as brain activation. Understanding brain activities is simple, but the implications for putting are of the highest magnitude.

Instruments exist that somewhat accurately measure the activation impulses of the brain. Simply stated, electrodes that measure electrical current as brain waves are attached to the outside of the head.

These instruments provide information that suggests that in most people, most of the time, the activation in the brain is scattered. However, when a person begins to concentrate or focus on something with a high degree of intensity, the activation of the brain becomes more localized in a specific section of the brain. When the concentration or focus becomes so intense the individual enters a high state of consciousness known as the "zone" or "flow," the activation becomes pinpointed in a relatively small area. The "zone" or "flow" activation area is about the size of a dime, but varies in locations from person to person, i.e., in some individuals the localization occurs predominately on the left side, others, on the right, and still others in the front or rear. People can be taught how to control this brain activation. In other words, people can be taught how to improve their concentration and focus, which in turn, improves their performance. You will demonstrate this for yourself by determining the location of the activation of your own brain and the intensity of its firing by taking the PeopleWise® Self-Assessment System found in Chapter 9. You will also be given a system for charting and monitoring your own putting performance that will help you determine the effectiveness of brain science. The charting and monitoring system is found at the end of Chapter 8.

The control of the firing of the brain is the key that unlocks the door to the subconscious. Consider for a moment the two functions of the subconscious: automatic and learned. The automatic function happens without thought: heartbeat, circulation, breathing, digestion, and other bodily functions. As presented in the previous two chapters, the learned function takes over automatically as a habit is formed: tying shoelaces, walking, speaking, memorizing, driving, riding a bicycle, adding, subtracting, multiplying, dividing, reading, etc. The word "habit" originally meant garment or clothing. This gives us an insight into the true meaning of habit. Our habits are literally garments worn by us. They fit and over time become a part of us. Masterful putting can become a habit when the subconscious is properly programmed.

Before, we talked about the interaction and role of the conscious and subconscious when catching a ball. Now let's elevate the complexity of catching a ball. The brain has to do a lot of complex things for a successful catch. Now complicate the matter by having the person run to get to the ball to catch it. Now distract the person by having people yell and scream. Finally, fill the subconscious with degrading comments to the point the person believes they are of little worth, are unsuccessful, and can't do anything right. When an individual gets into the "zone," he or she is able to screen out all the junk and screen in only those things that are necessary for a successful catch and do so this unconsciously. The goal is to achieve Olympian focus. Olympian focus just doesn't happen. Olympian focus is learned by influencing the subconscious through the controlling of the firing of the brain. Up to this point, we have intentionally kept the conscious part of the brain out of the way so the subconscious part could self-adjust and self-correct. Brain science shows us how we can consciously heighten our brain's firing in the subconscious to achieve even higher levels of performance.

During brain surgery, studies report that patients whose brain cells are stimulated with thin electrodes describe reliving scenes from the past. Keep in mind they are not remembering; they are reliving the experiences. When you control the firing of the brain, you experience sensations that allow you to "post-live." In other words, you create the future rather than relive the past. When you "post-live," you experience wholeheartedly before it happens. — You "will" it to happen. People that get into the "zone" are actually post-living, that is, they are seeing, feeling and experiencing the future events before it happens. In other words, they create the future.

Most scientists today agree that the functions of the brain cannot be simply compartmentalized as right- or left-brain dominant. Functions frequently appear in both hemispheres at the same time, but for most people the right side of the brain seems holistic, intuitive, and nonverbal while the left appears temporal, analytic, and verbal.

Researchers Amy Haufler and Bradley Hatfield in their videotape, *Math Like You Have Never See It Before*, narrated by Danny Glover, contend the left side of the brain is verbal, the right side is space and movement, the front is emotional, and the rear is visual. They have studied skilled and novice rifle shooters. By placing electrodes on the skull they measure brain waves simultaneously with the accuracy of rifle shots. Basically, they have concluded: novice shooters' brain activation is scattered; skilled shooters' brain activation is localized; and in Olympian shooters, five seconds before trigger pull, the firing of the brain is even more pinpointed than in skilled shooters, indicating superior focus and concentration.

By demonstrating to shooters how the brain activation relates to the accuracy of the shots, improvement in shooting is experienced. In other words, as one trains the body, one trains the mind. By mastering the mechanics of putting without conscious thought, coupled with controlling the brain through visual imagery and mental rehearsal, and now incorporating what we know about the activation of the brain through brain science, we can reverse the process — as one trains the mind, one trains the body.

You start to learn a physical skill through trial and error. You usually learn a few basics; then you practice, practice, practice. As you get better, it becomes a habit. The habit is predominantly controlling the learned function of the subconscious. What separates the good player from the excellent player is mostly mental. The excellent player just seems to "will" it to happen. Also, the excellent player doesn't let failures bother them as him or her as the good player.

You are shooting a free throw in basketball, and you are doing well. All of a sudden, you shoot an air ball. When you get ready to shoot after the air ball, it is hard to get the bad shot out of your mind. You keep mentally seeing the ball missing the rim, and you imagine people laughing at you, so you try to consciously force or guide the shot. What has happened is the subconscious has taken hold of you and the only thing you think you can control is the conscious part of your brain. The subconscious always wins over the conscious. The subconscious leads you to the rock in the road. Same thing with golf. You miss a putt, and all of a sudden you get the "yips." You try to consciously guide or force the ball in the hole. It is all the same. The subconscious controls our behavior as we try to out conscious the subconscious.

Or you have a successful string going and you realize you are going to set a personal best. All of a sudden you get overly anxious, overly sensitive, overly everything. What has happened is the subconscious has taken over to tell you enough is enough, get back into your picture of being who you really think you are. Get back into your comfort zone.

What we know now goes beyond the simple mind control of visual imagery and mental rehearsal. We know we can go directly to controlling the firing of our brain and control the subconscious by realizing where our brain fires naturally. The first step in grasping brain science is to understand the four theoretical areas of the brain and how they relate to us.

Understanding the Four Areas of the Brain

Some players putt more aggressively than others. Some jam the ball into the cup while others let it die in the hole. During the pre-shot routine some take more time than others. Different people approach the same thing in different ways. One person wants just to get the job done while the other wants to think on it, meditate about it, and consider options. One spouse wants to eat; the other wants to dine. One wants to buy; the other wants to shop. One wants sex; the other wants romance. People have the same wants and needs but their thinking and approaches to fulfilling those needs vary.

It is important to have a psychological match between how people learn with how they are taught. It is important to match expectations with approaches. The late Dr. Clare W. Graves, professor, Union College at Schenectady, New York, found an elegant pattern that relates people's thinking with their behaviors. He identifies a series of comfort zones referred to as Levels of Psychological Existence. Each Level has an optimal learning system. The relevance of Graves work to PeopleWise® Putting is directly related to Levels 4, 5, 6, and 7. By combining the work of Dr. Graves with current brain research findings, a case can be made that Level 4 brains function predominantly in the left hemisphere, Level 5 brains in the right, Level 6 in the front and Level 7 in the rear.

The entire PeopleWise® Series is based on understanding how the brain develops and functions. The foundation for PeopleWise® is formed from the work of Dr. Graves. Persons interested in a more detailed account of PeopleWise® may consult the first book of the PeopleWise® Series, *PeopleWise® Brain to Brain*.

The concept of Levels doesn't mean certain repertoires of behaviors. Rather Levels represent ways of thinking about things. Levels look at how choices are made not the choices themselves. The description of a Level tells us how people think and indicates why they might act a certain way.

Once we understand the *how's* and *why's*, the *what's* become predictable. The Levels tell us what kind of educational system and what sort of structure is the most effective. Levels tell how the individual wants to be treated, taught, managed and motivated.

Levels are like language lessons. We learn how to speak in terms that matter to the person. We help them find the motivators that work for them, so they can learn the most with the least energy. Not everyone learns the same things the same way. Most people are a mixture of Levels but have a preference of how they want to be handled, how to learn or how to think. When we understand how people think — get into their head so to speak — we not only understand them better, but we can help them learn.

Level 4: Absolutist

Self-sacrifice is the order of the day. There is a belief in a right way and a wrong way. Righteous deeds should be rewarded and transgressions should be punished. Maintaining discipline requires lots of energy for a Level 4. Level 4 thinking is absolutist thinking.

The values of hard work, commitment, and dutifulness fit the Level 4 mindset. One is expected to do the best one can. When Level 4 thinking is applied to work we ordinarily think of the Puritan work ethic. Respect abounds for those who work long, hard hours and who work their way up to earn what they have through the honest sweat of their brows. One must pay the price.

When dealing with Level 4 thinkers, it is important to recognize the importance of lists, rules and standard operating procedures. Things are best done in sequence — first things first. Too many variables lead to confusion in the mind.

Loyalty to a technique or procedure, as well as devotion, is characteristic of Level 4. Learning occurs from respected individuals who are experts. Cookbook approaches work. Tell it like it is; put it down in logical steps to be followed; and evaluate it right or wrong. People operating at this Level prefer practical things to abstract theory, matter of fact approaches to ambiguity and doubt.

Tight structure, linear sequences, regimentation, and limits are necessary.

Level 4 individuals learn best when there are no surprises. They learn best through a step-by-step method. They look for the best way. They go by the book.

An important part of Level 4 thinking is respect for authority figures. Those in authority are expected to look the part, dress the part and act accordingly. For insight into the Level 4 brain, let me share some of my "4-ness."

> I once had to fly to a small town to give a lecture. For the last leg, I was transferred to a little eight-seat aircraft. I'd never been in a plane this small before. As I got in and buckled, up, I looked forward and found there was no bulkhead. The pilot's seats and instrument panel with all its gauges and gadgets were right there, out in plain sight. It looked very complex and for a second or two I was frightened.

> When the lump in my throat settled, I looked around and found I was the only passenger. The pilot boarded, introduced himself as "Jerry," and clumsily settled into the left seat. He comfortingly advised me, "Don't worry. This won't take long. We'll be up and down before you know it."

> Although I have to fly a lot on large commercial airlines, I thought this was unique, a little too unique. What really bothered me was that "Jerry" wasn't in a uniform. He was wearing a hunting jacket and baseball cap with a patch on the cap that said, "Pilots get high in the sky." It was just too much for me. I unbuckled my seat belt, told "Jerry" there'd been a change in plans, and deplaned.

For all I know, he may have been an excellent pilot and it might have been a fine flight. But when I pay the prices they charge to fly today, I want a pilot in a uniform I can trust. I prefer to hand my life over to somebody who conforms to my Level 4 expec tations. The bus ride was excellent, by the way. The driver was wearing a well-pressed uniform and a proper sort of cap.

PeopleWise® Putting addresses Level 4 thinkers with respect and dignity. We lay it on the line in simple to understand language, and we show how to measure individual skill development. We not only know what we are talking about, we also dress appropriately.

Level 5: Materialist

Level 5 thinkers see options, alternatives and possibilities all around. They relish change and novelty. When the Level 5 mind is activated, people start thinking in cause-and-effect terms — if you do A, B will probably happen. They believe they cause things to happen; they make their own breaks; and they are responsible for their own destinies. Level 5 thinkers mold, change and develop their environments. They act and pro-act rather than react or accept.

Accountability is big at Level 5. Individuals are responsible for their own actions. Thinking is result oriented, outcome based, and evaluative. Nice tries don't count.

Motion-through-space analysis is characteristic of Level 5 think-ing. Motion-through-space refers to objectively determining the positioning of a thing relative to others in a given situation. An example is, you can tell the success of individuals by the cars they drive or the houses they live in. In a Level 5 business, you can measure people's importance by observing their offices. Beginners with low status are placed in an office pool where they share sup-plies and equipment with others. Next, they may get a personal space complete with credenza and bookshelves. An office over-looking the work pool comes next, then one with a window on to the parking lot. A wooden desk replaces metal, carpet appears, and there is the possibility of an adjoining restroom and conference facilities. To a Level 5, the golf equipment is not only important; it affects one's attitude toward the game. As they say, the Level 5 likes to look good getting off the bus.

In football, decals on helmets indicating number of tackles may motivate a Level 5. Charts and graphs that show progress help maintain interest and provide incentive to put forth more effort.

Level 5 is calculating. They weigh probabilities and then rationally approach challenges in ways that achieve results. One asset available at Level 5 is multiplistic thinking — the ability to handle many things at once, keep several irons in the fire, and juggle several things simultaneously.

The Level 5 not only wants results. They want data. They use the data to generalize and extrapolate from. They want to know why something works, and they have an appreciation for theory and conjecture. They like to get at the root of the problem. They want to know why something works or doesn't work.

PeopleWise® Putting addresses Level 5 thinkers by explaining not only how to do it but why it works. Simply put, PeopleWise® Putting is logical, makes sense, and it works. You prove its effectiveness by measuring your own progress.

Comparing and contrasting Levels 4 and 5 clarify the differences between the two. The Level 4 prefers a controlled, deliberate and fairly predictable situation while the Level 5 likes change, novelty and risk. A Level 5 tends to be active and assertive; a Level 4 is more reserved. Level 4 thinkers are often perfectionists, accurate, digitized and focused while Level 5 thinkers lock on to the success of winning, not details or learning the rules.

While the Level 4 is trying to take care of obligations, the Level 5 is laying plans to get better. Level 4 thinkers tend to hear and remember every detail of a conversation while Level 5 thinkers are "selective listeners" who hear and remember what they want to hear, predominantly what they agree with.

A Level 4 likes precise directions while a Level 5 just wants to be pointed in the right direction. Level 4 people can accept a compliment while Level 5 people may thrive on a compliment. A Level 4 does what is expected, a Level 5 does what is necessary to stay ahead. A Level 4 is territorial, that is to say they like their space and their own things; a Level 5 has no boundaries and will use anyone's stuff if it will help get the job done.

A Level 4 will move deliberately at a slow pace while a Level 5 is quick and sometimes abrupt. Level 4 holds back; Level 5 jumps ahead. Level 4 demonstrates loyalty; Level 5 takes command. Level 4 concentrates on the task at hand by doing one thing at a time; Level 5 sets goals and forms a strategy. Level 4 thinkers see things in black and white; Level 5 thinkers like to dabble in the grays.

The Level 4 and 5 admire the legendary football coach, Vince Lombardi, but for different reasons. Lombardi advocated the hard work, self-sacrifice, blood, sweat and tears that the Level 4 brain hits on. He also insisted on winning as "the only thing," and the thrill of victory is what stimulates the Level 5 brain.

Level 4 motivations involve rules, policies, security, custom, and order. Level 5 is concerned with incentives, rewards, advancement, competitive edge, motion-through-space, data gathering, and evaluation.

As you can see, these two Levels have two different mindsets, and for learning to become permanent and for the putting stroke to be repeatable, the practice methods need to be in concert with the individual's thinking and disposition. PeopleWise® Putting not only addresses these differences, it capitalizes on them.

Level 6: Sociocentric

Level 6 people are interested in affiliation, acceptance, and understanding one's self. This way of thinking is empathetic and sensitive, self-disclosing and deeply concerned with feelings. Level 6 thinking includes spontaneity, loose structure, and permissiveness. Level 6 people want harmony and agreement.

People functioning at Level 6 learn best through observation and involvement. Level 6 people learn from others, especially if they like them and feel comfortable around them. They learn best and most from those they trust. Level 6 individuals, for the most part, question experts and persons of authority.

Since friendship, tolerance, and sincerity are important values, Level 6 thinkers do not respond well to traditional instruction that is regimented or reinforcement based. Resistance is encountered to directive teaching, structured situations, and task-oriented projects. They rebel when treated as a number or by the book.

Nondirective techniques, involvement, and participation work well with Level 6 thinking. It is important to get a "sense-of-the-idea" or a "feeling-for-the-task."

Level 6 individuals believe that answers lie within themselves, so they may spend time in introspection and meditation. Self-discovery is key.

For the Level 6, PeopleWise® Putting allows opportunities for self-discovery and self-awareness. Ideas for experimenting are offered, and self-judgment is encouraged. Emphasis is placed on methods and processes while objective results are de-emphasized.

Level 7: Cognitive

Although the number of Level 7 thinkers is few, we are finding that more and more individuals are beginning to develop their Level 7 faculties. Level 7 individuals are internally driven and have conquered fear. They have no fear of boss, survival, social acceptance, or even death. Most Level 7 people have either had a close encounter with death or have experienced someone close to them die.

Level 7 thinkers are in a state of autonomy, inner-directedness, high functionality, and cognizant complexity. They have confidence in their ability and believe they are somewhat unlimited if and when they set out to do something.

From the Level 7 perspective, nothing is universally right or wrong, good or bad. Everything is judged within its context. Things are good or bad in terms of their impact on overall processes, long-range implications, and the best information available.

Evaluation is internalized and there is nothing to prove. Failure is a learning experience. Success is based on self-perceived ranges of what is possible versus what actually happened. There will be explanation and analysis but rarely excuses or fault finding. Sometimes naively honest and discomfortingly straightforward, thinking at Level 7 is never ego-defensive or deceitful.

Level 7 thinkers are at peace with themselves. There is no master plan. Everything is a movement, and all movements are interesting. Level 7 thinkers want to make the most out of every movement and sometimes this leads to an appearance of childlike (not childish) behavior, uninhibitedness, and spontaneity.

Level 7 thinking is complex. Awareness is heightened to the point that insignificant things take on significance not to the task or situation, but significant to the Level 7 mind.

> One day I was having lunch with a Level 7 person at the local "greasy spoon." We were sitting at the counter when suddenly, out of the blue, he leaned over and said enthusiastically, "Look at that!"

I looked around, couldn't see anything, and went back to my burger.

My friend was staring at the grill. I looked to where he was staring and only saw the grease-stained covering over the exhaust fan. I asked, "What are you talking about?"

"That Formica over the grill," he replied. "Isn't that outstanding?"

All I saw was a disgusting blue panel with pink and brown streaks. To the Level 7 brain, it was a study in patterns and contrasts, wearing the stories of a million burgers and a zillion fries. The Formica was a mosaic of diner-ness to my friend, to me, it was more worthy of a call to the Health Department than the Museum of Modern Art.

While a Level 4 sees beauty in historic relics, a Level 5 values precious antiques and a Level 6 appreciates the naturalness of old wood with is beautiful grain and patina, the Level 7 finds meaning in Formica, plastic, and Plexiglas. Level 7 thinkers may appear to be living ahead of their time, or at least to be out of sync with most everyone else.

When asked why they do things, people at Level 7 say, "Because I chose to...," "I wanted to...," or "Since it was what needed to be done..." These motivators take precedence over material gain, prestige, recognition, the need to be liked, rules or other's expectations. One acts because one has decided to.

Level 7 functioners seem to get the most out of life, milking every ounce of events, activities and happenings. The famous psychologist and author, Abraham Maslow, refers to this skill as being involved in a peak experience. Level 7 living involves a series of peak experiences throughout almost all activities. Maslow used the Japanese Zen-based word muga for this awareness of the present moment. It is a state of experiencing something wholeheartedly, totally, without thinking of anything else, but just being without hesitation, inhibition, or fear of criticism. Time matters at Level 7 but not scheduled time or efficiency in time. Control of one's time is the key, whether it be to think, play, work, create, meditate, and that control will not be surrendered to outside forces. The Level 7 person is not driven by the clock or imposed schedules. Response to schedules is a matter of choice, not compulsion.

Have you ever become so involved and interested in something that you almost lose track of what else is going on? That is somewhat like Level 7 type thinking, except the Level 7 doesn't lose touch. One is highly focused and generally aware at the same time.

Those at Level 4 reminisce about the past; Level 5s set goals and strategies for the future; and Level 6s strive to get in touch with the here-and-now. Level 7s aren't aligned with past, present or future; there's no need to fight the cosmos. Level 7s are interested in process.

Level 4s question if there is life after death. Level 7s determine where there is life after *birth*. And they proceed to experience it to supernatural heights.

Since Level 7s have much to contribute but refuse to be told how to do things, PeopleWise® Putting passes on what we have learned from Level 7s and encourages them to continue to explore and experiment with new ideas, styles, methods, and concepts.

You have mastered the basics, and you have mastered mind control. You are beginning to understand brain science. Now it is time to become a PeopleWise® putter and attain the status of being a *real, real* good putter.

CHAPTER 8
PeopleWise® Putting

I once had an opportunity to advise a discus thrower on the track team at the University of Virginia. He came to me because in practice he performed extremely well, but during a meet he seemed to choke up and fouled constantly. A PeopleWise® analysis found that he was a Level 6 who was practicing like a Level 4. He had a favorite discus (Level 4 thinking), and he carried it everywhere with him. He felt this discus was a part of him, sort of an extension of his body. This type of thinking is healthy for a Level 4, but a Level 6 who gets a favorite discus begins to get the idea that a great deal of the distance thrown is related to the discus itself. Sure enough, I found that when given two other identical discuses, he always threw his favorite discus the farthest.

My job was simple. I had to convince him that *he* was the important element in the process of throwing the discus. I did this by taking his favorite discus away and providing him with three identical discuses of different colors: one red, one orange, and one blue. Each day, he would throw each discus three times, with all distances recorded. Afterwards, he would practice as usual, but not with his favorite discus. Over a period of three weeks, he was shown that no particular discus was superior. In other words, I wanted him to realize that *he* was in complete control of throwing the discus: the discus itself was irrelevant. I wanted him to build confidence in himself to such a degree that he would know *he could throw* any discus, rock, hammer, or plate farther than anyone.

As he began to realize that his personal talent was responsible for his success, he was given his favorite discus back. He quickly found that he threw it as far but no farther than the others. He won the next meet, set two school records, and most importantly, he never fouled once for the rest of the season.

Obviously, I was working with a very talented athlete who had superior physical talent, but for some reason, became distracted or would psych himself out during a meet. He was psychologically, emotionally, and intellectually healthy, and if it were legal to count or measure his performance in practice, without competition, he would not have needed any motivational help. However, when he was in a meet he would put pressure on himself. Just prior to throwing the discus he would consciously try to control his focus, but his subconscious would override the conscious and distract him to such a degree he would choke up and foul. In other words, his subconscious was leading him to the rock in the road. When I discovered he had Level 6 tendencies, theoretically, his brain would naturally fire in the front part, but he practiced as a Level 4 using rigid repetition with the same discus, forcing his brain to fire in the left hemisphere. Thus, during a meet when it was paramount to optimize the firing of the brain in a small, localized area to obtain Olympian focus, he couldn't do it. The brain wanted to fire in the front, but he was forcing it to fire on the left side.

Whenever there is a battle between the conscious and the sub-conscious, the subconscious always wins. In his case, when the discus thrower didn't put pressure on himself, he had great concentration. Over time, by practicing like a Level 4 through rigid, rigorous, persevering repetition, he learned to fire his brain in the left hemisphere. However, when the pressure was on, the front part of his brain competed with the left. Thus he became distracted because his brain could not screen out all the junk that was going on around him. By forcing him to practice using the front part of the brain, which was natural to him (being a Level 6), he became more confident in himself because the brain was firing more naturally. The result was, when the pressure was on, the brain fired wholeheartedly in the front without competition from the left hemisphere. Thus extraneous junk was screened out and the firing of the brain became pinpointed in the front, creating Olympian focus. Using standard mind-control techniques through visual imagery and mental rehearsal, it would have been possible to override the natural tendency for the front part of the brain to fire; however, this would have taken extraordinary time, energy, and practice.

By using PeopleWise® Putting we are able to short circuit the process and get results quicker, faster, and with less effort. Brain science doesn't try to make water run up hill. When using PeopleWise® Putting, instead of trying to force the process, we let the process happen naturally and effortlessly. PeopleWise® Putting will not work by making a strained, conscious effort. The secret of PeopleWise® Putting is to determine where the brain wants to fire most naturally and then align the practice methods accordingly. When this is done, you don't need to practice much.

> I used a similar strategy with a golfer when her putting went sour. This golfer had tendencies to be a 7. After learning about PeopleWise® Putting, she described golf as a multileveled game. She had determined that driving and long iron shots were Level 5 techniques, midirons were Level 4, while short irons and putting strokes were Level 6 techniques. She stated that golf is such a difficult game to master because psychologically you have to switch your mental preparation numerous times from 4 through 6.

She improved her putting (while practicing) by never putting a ball the same distance with the same club. She would use three different putters on the practice green. As she putted six practice balls, she would alternate her putters and, as mentioned earlier, she never putted a ball the same direction or distance. She claimed that a professional putter must develop a feel and sense for putting, so that when she is on the green she is confident that she can get the ball close to, if not in the hole. Furthermore, a professional putter knows she can hit it with any putter, or as explained in Chapter 1, with a Dr. Pepper bottle. Good putters master touch and feel — they exploit the Level 6 in themselves. A professional golfer does not have to be a Level 7. This Level 7 simply viewed the game from a PeopleWise® Putting standpoint and improved her putting by bringing out the 6 in herself.

A typical Level 4 approach to golf would be Tommy Armour's, *How to Play Your Best Golf All the Time*. In this classic book, one finds many rules regarding how to stand, how to position your elbow, etc. Most of the rules are numbered or are presented in lists. On the other hand, many of the tips on golfing found in *Golf Digest* appeal to Level 5s. Here we find suggestions from professionals that incorporate a cause and effect approach to understanding the game by looking at the swing in terms of weights, balances, arcs, and torque. We find Level 5 discussions on compression and the science of what happens to the ball on contact. The many product changes using different metals and aerodynamic designs are outgrowths of Level 5 thinking.

Level 6s enjoy playing golf, but most do not take the game seriously. Many are not competitive; they have been known to play a round barefooted; and they like to look at the beauty of the landscaping and breathe the clean air. Most 6s are good putters.

Level 4s have a regimented approach to the game and play one shot at a time. Level 5s plan a strategy for playing a round as well as a strategy for hitting the ball, while Level 6s just like being outdoors. Often Level 5s take pride in how fast they play a round — they've decided that it is a game of speed. Level 5s enjoy hitting into a foursome of 6s. The 6s enjoy the scenery and, when pushed on the golf course, exhibit a little passive resistance. That is, they intentionally slow down just enough to make things really unpleasant for the people behind them. As a result, the 5s hit into them; the 6s get mad and scream a little. Then the 5s grumble and curse while they drive their cart past them. All in all, it seems to be good therapy; everyone's pent-up aggressions are released; and there is an element of psychological healthiness involved in yelling at those you don't know.

The previous paragraph is somewhat sarcastic and written for the most part jokingly with tongue-in-cheek, but in reality it isn't too far off from the truth. After testing and interviewing more than one hundred weekend golfers, we have found that different PeopleWise® Levels exhibit specific habits, characteristics, beliefs, and behaviors directly related to their Level. We determined each golfer's Level of functioning by administering the PeopleWise® Profile System similar to the instrument presented in the next chapter, Chapter 9. We asked each golfer to give us words that would describe them and we validated the words with descriptions given to us by their competitors and partners. We observed their play and talked with them about how they approached the game, their beliefs and philosophies, and historically, how they got started.

Left Brain Dominant, Level 4, Absolutist	
Disciplined	Regimented
Methodical	Hard on Self
Persistent	Steady
Controlled	Single-Minded

Practicing using the same technique over and over and over until your hands get numb. Practice makes perfect. Looking for "the" method or technique. Methodical approach, incremental, step-by-step.

The crowd behind the 18th green cheered as the leader's approach shot smacked into the turf. The ball took two hops and then reversed under the effects of backspin, finishing three feet from the flag. The leader, now with three strokes to victory, walked briskly on to the green and deliberately clipped the ball into a bunker with his putter. He splashed the ball back out to the green and, with his usual perfunctory glance along the line, stroked it into the hole (Dobereiner, 1991, p. 176). Such are the many tales of Moe Norman.

> Moe Norman, the founder of Natural Golf, has been classified as a savant of golf. He has earned the reputation of being the best ball striker in the history of the game of golf. He developed his own technique of hitting the ball the same way each and every time, much like a machine. After watching him play for more than two years (never being out of the fairway) an observer noticed he had used the same tee. When asked, "Do you realize you've used the same tee for two and a half years?" His reply was, "Aren't you supposed to?"

> In July 2001, I was attending my first Natural Golf Clinic in New Orleans. It was a beautiful day. The air smelled crisp and clean, and the temperature was perfect. I was waiting with three other students outside the clubhouse. We knew a little about Moe Norman from a television infomercial, and we were anxious to learn this new simplified way of hitting a golf ball. The Master Instructor, Tom Sanders, was a protégé of Moe Norman and had an excellent reputation of being a lot like Moe and

an expert ball striker himself. I'll never forget meeting Tom for the first time. He came around the corner of the clubhouse dragging his bag of clubs. He was sort of pear-shaped; his cap was on crooked; and his shirttail was out on the left-hand side. He introduced himself and promptly led us to the driving range, where there were four piles of balls. Each pile could easily have filled one-half of a fifty-five gallon drum barrel. I'd never seen so many balls in one place. He teed up two balls, pointed to the 200-yard sign, and announced he was going to hit the sign. He addressed the ball, looked at the sign, looked down at the ball and, without any hesitation, swung. The ball bounced off the metal 200-yard sign with a loud bang. Before we could say anything, he struck the second ball and it hit the sign with a "ker-thunk." The four of us, speechless, looked at each other in awe. Tom looked up at us and realized something was going on and asked, "Is there something wrong?" One of the students spoke out, "We've never seen that done before." Tom, the Master Instructor, looked at us matter-of-factly and uttered, "Well, it's a pretty big sign."

Next he showed us the baseball grip, how to swing (somewhat like hitting a hockey puck) and how to place the ball in the middle of our stance. For the next three hours, non-stop, we hit balls. Tom moved from student to student, saying the same thing over and over, while the attendant kept us in balls, lots of balls. We took thirty minutes for lunch and returned to hit balls for three more hours without break one. Regardless of club selection, your grip never changed, your swing never changed, and the ball placement never changed. That, my friends, was the clinic. This was a pure Level 4 clinic, conducted by a Level 4 instructor, using a Level 4 process, with a Level 4 philosophy. Instead of hitting balls 'til our hands got numb, we hit balls 'til they bled, and then we continued to hit balls while they kept bleeding.

Right Brain Dominant, Level 5, Materialist	
Assertive	Confident
Competitive	Bold
Doer	Decisive
Hard Driving	Aggressive

A student of the game. An avid reader of golf magazines and subscriber to the Golf Channel. Understands the strategies and physics of the game. Practice doesn't make perfect; perfect practice makes perfect. Attacks the course with a win at all costs attitude. Adrenalin charged using a grip-it and rip-at-it style.

Dave Pelz, president and founder of the Dave Pelz Short Game School, has established himself as the authority of understanding and teaching how to putt and hit short irons. My first Pelz Short Game Clinic took place in Tampa Bay, Florida, at the Westin Innisbrook Resort. The facilities were breathtaking. The morning started in an elegant conference room overlooking the golf course right after a complete breakfast with all the trimmings. There were four instructors who eventually broke us up into three groups of six students. The head instructor laid out the day's agenda and began to show statistics verifying the importance of the short game. Next — through the use of flip charts and graphics — tricks of the short game trade were explained and demonstrated, followed by each group going to the course to begin practicing. Each group went to a separate learning station, i.e., pitch, chip and sand. The groups rotated every thirty minutes. Teaching aids were used throughout — like a bunkerboard for hitting out of sand. The bunkerboard was beveled in the middle, placed in the sand, and a small mound of sand was put on the board with the ball placed on the mound of sand. With little practice you could hit under the ball and guide the ball on to the green. How the club hit the sand to make the ball explode out onto the green was explained much like a lab technician would explain a science experiment in a physics course. Lunch was elegant and very tasty. Following lunch we were introduced to Perfy, the putting robot. Perfy was used to show the physics of striking the ball perfectly. Next, we were introduced to the putting track, which helped monitor the exact pathway of the putter head from take away to follow through. From the putting track we moved to the truthboard. The truthboard had a mirror placed directly behind the ball. When you addressed the ball you should have been able to see your eyes in the mirror since good putters have their head directly over the ball — pretty clever and pretty 5ish.

This clinic had more gimmicks than it had students and the instruction was top-drawer. It was a pure Level 5 clinic, using Level 5 teaching aids by Level 5 instructors in their Level 5 color-coordinated golfing outfits. It was impressive, to say the least.

Forebrain Dominant, Level 6, Sociocentric	
Social	Casual
Tolerant	Caring
Patient	Companion
Relaxed	Non-Assertive

Golf is primarily for recreation and socialization. While golfing, take time to appreciate the environment, nature, and friends. The most important thing in golf is to enjoy and have fun as opposed to winning or beating someone. For the serious Level 6 player, golf is a game of touch, feel, and finesse.

The most unusual golf clinic I ever attended was advertised as "The Inner Game of Golf." The instructor was in his 50s, and about six feet tall. His hair hung to his shoulders and he was dressed in a short-sleeved, brightly decorated, Hawaiian shirt, jeans, docksiders, and no socks. It took place in Biloxi, Mississippi, at the old D'Iberville Hotel. There were only two other participants and myself. As part of the enrollment fee, we received M. Scott Peck's book, *Golf and the Spirit*. The theme throughout the day was, Golf is a Game of Life Where We Learn About Our Inner Strength.

The session started with all of us removing our shoes and socks. We sat on the floor, and we began to learn how to lower anxiety through proper breathing exercises. We would inhale through our nose, hold for six seconds, and exhale through our mouth while touching the tip of our tongue to the upper back of our front teeth. It sounds crazy, but after about ten deep inhales with forced exhales, I began to get lightheaded and somewhat dizzy. Next, we did some stretching exercises.

After getting loosened up, each participant shared times while playing golf that were aggravating, unpleasant, and stressful. This was followed by a lecturette on our freedom to choose to be angry or not angry, frustrated or not frustrated. It was explained that no golf ball, golf event, or golf situation could make a person angry unless the individual allowed it to make them angry. We can choose to allow ourselves to be angry or not angry.

Next, we began to explore ways to proact as opposed to react to various golfing situations that might trigger frustration. We looked at various ways to play the game that might lower anxiety, like playing a scramble where team plays each player's best ball; providing multiple mulligans to even the skill levels; keeping a total group score and setting a goal to lower the group score by so much within a certain length of time as opposed to keeping individual scores.

Toward the middle of the afternoon, we were introduced to a blind person who demonstrated his ability to putt. The putting took place in the back of the conference room on the carpet. A cup was rigged up like you might find in someone's office. Even though he couldn't see, he was an excellent putter as long as he was told where and how far the cup was and, of course, when he missed, where the ball ended up. We were taught that when the blind use a mobility walking cane they actually sense the tip of the cane as if it were an extended finger.

Each of us was blindfolded and taught the basics of mobility training using a cane and getting a feel for the tip as we tapped around the room. Next, the putter was substituted for the cane as we moved about the room. Finally, the blindfolds were removed, and after some brief instruction on putting, we began to learn how to lag to a line, putt through a bridge made of play LEGO blocks, and finally, into the rigged-up cup. We were all surprised at how our putting improved as we learned to view the putter as an extension of our hands and fingers.

Although the clinic was more like a workshop, it definitely was conducted like a Level 6 program, by a Level 6 instructor, with a Level 6 theme running throughout the day.

Rear Brain Dominant, Level 7, Cognitive

Innovative	Flair
Adventuresome	Joust & Joke
Fearless	Experiment
Inquiring	Aura

Self-evaluation of performance is unrelated to the score. One may evaluate performance as very well, yet score poorly, or one may evaluate performance as terrible, yet beat everybody and score extremely well. Talk to self and then answer back. Adjusts rapidly during a game. When hot, will run a birdie-streak like a professional.

Out of the 100+ samples we interviewed, we only ended up with four individuals we could identify as Level 7s. Each one reported having more than two holes in one. Every hole in one was reported as happening on a misty day, and they felt strange, as if they were a different person, as if someone inside of them hit the ball in the hole. All reported from time to time they tried to hit the ball differently. They would step into the ball like a batter in baseball, run and hit the ball, double swing in two full circles before hitting the ball or hit the ball from a crouched-down position as opposed to a standing upright position. All four Level 7 golfers had single-digit handicaps, but they didn't play regularly; once a week at best.

We've never been to a Level 7 golf clinic and we've never heard of one, but we imagine the new millennium will bring Level 7 golfers with Level 7 approaches to the game. When it happens, we imagine they will not look like golfers, play like golfers, or act like golfers, but they will revolutionize the game as we know it today.

The golf clinic that left the greatest impression on me and has revolutionized the game for me was conducted by Tim and Todd Graves. The Graves Golf Academy is located in Oklahoma City, Oklahoma. But my first exposure to the Graves training took place south of Mobile, Alabama in December 2001 on a very cold and windy day. The Graves method teaches the Natural Golf approach founded by Moe Norman. Tim is referred to as "Little Moe." What is so impressive about the Graves teaching method is that it appeals to both male and female of all ages from teen to senior, offers a wide range of skills from beginner to professional, and incorporates techniques for Levels 4, 5, and 6. Level 4s are drawn to the simplified mechanics of the swing and the professional demonstration by Tim. Level 5s are impressed with the sophisticated instruction utilizing video feedback incorporating cause and effect thinking. Level 6s respond to the individualized attention that makes every participant feel important and as if the instructors care. During the session on the cold and windy day, Todd personally brought piping hot cocoa to each participant on the driving range while Tim was demonstrating the Natural Golf swing. The consistent and timely follow up of electronic newsletters at no cost to the participants is appreciated by all three Levels. It was at the workshop that I was exposed to stringing an eight-foot fishing line between gutter spikes that is explained in Chapter 3, Nuts and

Bolts. All participants, including me, found this teaching aid to make sense and to be effective in helping to improve everyone's putting regardless of their preference in level of instruction.

Now is the time we put the frosting on the cake. We are going to take everything we have learned up to this point and we're going to put it into a procedure that will allow you to control the firing of your own brain. As you attain the skill of firing your own brain, you will develop Olympian confidence and focus that will improve any physical skill you choose. You are on the brink of becoming a PeopleWise® putter who is real, real good.

Brain science is new. We have learned more about the brain in the past five years than in the past one hundred. Historically, nearly 90 percent of all neuroscientists are alive today. It is always tempting to take research findings out of context and look for simplistic solutions to complex problems.

PeopleWise® Putting will be viewed by some as an oversimplification of hemispheric dominance. Keep in mind, PeopleWise® Putting is a theory and not necessarily the truth. However, you can test this theory to determine if it works for you. We will present the procedure for applying PeopleWise® Putting in a format that is understandable and immediately applicable and then we will show you a way to test the theory to determine if it works for you. The genius of PeopleWise® is in its simplicity, and the beauty is in its direct usage. Some claim there are no quick fixes, but PeopleWise® Putting is so powerful you will see improvement in your skill development in less than a month. The improvement is visible and measurable and permanent.

Peoplewise® Putting relies heavily on two assumptions: (a) the brain is physiologically affected by the environment and (b) emotion plays a major role on the impact of the brain. Ronald Kotulak, in his book *Inside the Brain*, uses a metaphor of a banquet to illustrate the interaction of the brain and the environment.

> The brain gobbles up the external environment through its sensory system and then reassembles

the digested world in the form of trillions of connections which are constantly growing or dying,
becoming stronger or weaker depending on the
richness of the banquet. (p. 4)

Peoplewise® Putting feeds the brain highly specialized nutritious environmental food, which supercharges its firing in specified targets. This ultimately leads to Olympian confidence and focus. Marian Diamond introduced the concept of "neural plasticity." Neural plasticity is the brain's ability to constantly change its structure and function in response to external experiences. To assist in structurally altering the brain, PeopleWise® Putting supplies a steady stream of environmental vitamins that enhance localized explosions and reduce randomized and scattered firing of the brain. The brain is essentially curious and Peoplewise® Putting capitalizes on this curiosity by helping the brain make connections between the unknown, to the known — between the attempt, to successful skill execution.

The brain is strongly influenced by emotion. Daniel Goleman's *Emotional Intelligence* and Joseph LeDoux's *The Emotional Brain* have helped us understand the role of emotion on learning. Simply stated, the stronger the emotion connected with an experience, the stronger the memory of the experience. Add emotion into learning, and the brain deems the information more important and retention is increased. PeopleWise® Putting uses the "emotional key" to unlock the subconscious. In skill development, the subconscious always wins out over the conscious. The trick to firing your own brain is to unlock the subconscious, so you control it and it doesn't control you.

Why is it that during the last two minutes of a football game the offense seems to play with greater intensity and concentration? Why is it that during the last thirty seconds of a basketball game, the percentage of completed shots substantially increases from the previous part of the game? Might it not be that the players are more focused, more excited, more emotional? What is causing the emotion? Is it the environmental circumstances, like the fans are yelling louder, the clock is ticking, the coach and players are in unity as to exactly what must be done, the heart is pumping faster, or the adrenalin is flowing more freely? When the touchdown is made, and/or the basketball rips the net, does it take longer to quiet down? Just maybe, emotion plays a significant role in getting the brain to fire in a small, localized part of the brain that enhances an individual's concentration and focus. What PeopleWise® Putting does, it allows you to control the emotion rather than wait for the environment to capture it. When you take charge of injecting emotional probes into your brain, you control the firing, but as we learned from Clare Graves, not all emotional probes are the same for everyone. PeopleWise® Putting allows us to determine which emotional probe stimulates our brain the best.

Here is where the rubber meets the road. We are going to lay out the procedure for firing your own brain. Anyone who plays golf knows that games are won and lost on the putting green, yet the average player will not practice putting for any given length of time. Players will endlessly hit balls on a driving range or even chip and pitch buckets of balls on a green or at a target, but they won't devote even a quarter of the time to putting.

Why is it that something as important as putting is so distasteful? Because it is boring, that's why. PeopleWise® Putting may not put any joy into practicing putting, but it will provide a system for showing you how to practice putting that will efficiently increase your putting skill and provide an accurate feedback loop that assures success with minimal effort using minimal practice time.

As we show you how to control the firing of your own brain, we assume you have reasonable coordination, and you have somewhat mastered the basics. At this time, you convincingly see yourself as a good putter. Without consciously thinking you keep your head still, hit the ball on the sweet spot, and your pendulum stroke keeps the club head square and on the aimline path. To make PeopleWise® Putting work, you don't have to be a professional; you just need to be able to reasonably execute the skill.

Left Brain Dominant, Level 4, Absolutist

Your strength lies in perseveration, methodical approach, incremental steps, step-by-step process. You will use a SEE-DO process.

You begin by placing the ball about where you are 60 percent successful. For you, four to six feet from the hole. You grip the club exactly the way you want; you address the ball exactly the way you want; you look at the cup and then refocus on the ball. You imagine the ball dropping into the cup. You hear the plunk of the ball dropping into the bottom of the cup. At this point you experience joy and a tingling sensation. After reveling in the successful experience you strike the ball. As the ball drops in, you get a double charge of emotion. When you miss, flush it out of your mind quickly and begin again. When you practice, make sure you are at a distance where you are at least 60 percent successful. As you control the firing of your brain in the left hemisphere you will improve your skill. When you get at 90 percent accuracy, move back six inches. When you get at the distance when it is unreasonable to make the ball go into the hole, make the hole bigger by drawing a chalk line around the hole. Now your target is to get within the chalk line. At fifteen to twenty feet, mentally shoot for getting the ball inside the leather and beyond twenty feet get the ball within one club-length around the hole.

It is very important that while practicing you never get beyond the distance where your accuracy level falls below 60 percent. Your strength is in the repeated firing of your brain, which explodes every time you use this procedure and hit your target. If you are at a distance that drops below 50 percent, you are confusing the subconscious. To make PeopleWise® Putting work for you, you must see the ball hit the target, feel it, *then* strike it, and when it goes in 60 percent of the time or better the firing of the brain records what the muscles and nervous system did for repeated performance. For you, practice makes perfect.

SEE — you mentally see the ball go into the hole and hear the plunk as it drops to the bottom of the cup, which sends joy throughout your body and, after experiencing the tingling feeling; you DO — by striking the ball.

Using the SEE-DO process, making sure you feel the emotion *before* executing the skill, you will experience success that can be objectively determined with very little practice. If you do not experience improvement, then you either cannot generate the necessary emotional excitement *prior* to execution or you are not a Level 4.

Right Brain Dominant, Level 5, Materialist

Your strength lies in your cause and effect type of thinking and your intense drive to make it happen. You will use a TUBE process. By using the TUBE process, you will trick your brain into firing in the right hemisphere by being logical and cognitive.

You would rather do anything but putt, yet your brain activates in such a way you can learn to control the firing of your brain very quickly and improve your putting with minimal effort and practice. For you, practice doesn't make perfect. Perfect practice makes perfect or perfect practice makes permanent.

To utilize the TUBE technique for putting, you place two ball markers six inches from the cup the width of the cup. A ball placed six feet from the cup is now only five feet, six inches. You are tricking your mind into believing the hole is closer. You imagine the ball markers making a six-inch tube to the hole. You imagine the ball going through the tube; you hear the plunk, which makes you tingle with excitement, then you stroke the ball. You will experience immediate success, and you will be tempted to move the ball further away from the hole. Don't. Stay at the six-feet distance with the markers six inches from the hole, and concentrate on experiencing the emotion *prior* to striking the ball. When you feel you are controlling the emotion on a consistent regular basis, begin to move the ball back in six-inch increments. Within a very short period of time you will be knocking down seven and eight footers. As with the SEE-DO procedure, when you get at the distance it is unreasonable to make the ball go into the hole (making less than 60 percent of the putts), make the hole bigger by drawing a chalk line around the hole. At fifteen to twenty feet, mentally target a hole with a radius within the leather and beyond twenty feet the radius is one club length. You will naturally want to extend the tube by moving the ball markers farther from the hole. Moving the marker farther back from the hole works for some Level 5s better than others. You are a cognitive person. You think cause and effect. You will figure out what works best for you, and believe me, you will experience success within a very short period of time with minimal practice. Your challenge is to make yourself see the tube, hear the plunk, and feel the tingle *before* striking the ball. You must make your conscious outsmart your subconscious.

What is interesting with Level 5s is, as they experiment with the movement of the markers soon they are able to just imagine the markers. The physical placement of the markers is no longer needed. At this point the Level 5 is consciously controlling the activation of the brain.

The danger is, the Level 5s get so good so fast they forget to wait for the emotion before striking the ball. The key to controlling the activation of the brain is feeling the excitement of converting it before the ball is struck.

In golf, you must realize you can stroke a ball perfectly, and you might miss because of an imperfection in the green. A cleat mark, small bump, or indentation can play havoc with a putt. If you strike the ball perfectly and the ball doesn't go in, you flush out the subconscious by consciously reprimanding the green, "That damn spot, it moved my ball." Remember, you are intelligent and you are smart enough to know when it's the green's fault. So, don't consciously try to trick the subconscious into believing you are better than you are when you were perfect to begin with.

> Willie Masconi, the great pool shark, taught me this many years ago when he gave a demonstration at the recreational pool hall in Lawrence, Kansas. He

came in, chalked up, placed some balls on the table, and began to warm up. As I watched, he was phenomenal. After about five minutes, he was trying a finesse shot in the far right corner, but he kept barely missing it. After the fourth miss, he cursed out loud at the table, jammed his cue stick against the corner of the wall, stomped outside to his car, and returned with a carpenter's level. He placed the level on the table and the pool hall attendants were immediately summoned to put small shims under the corner pocket he kept missing. It might have been all for show, but it impressed me and everyone in the building. I don't remember him missing another shot that day.

You can't put a shim under a green, but sometimes it is the green's fault. So reprimand the green when and where appropriate.

Forebrain Dominant, Level 6, Sociocentric

Your strength lies in your sensitivity to others and the environment. Although not particularly competitive, you get a kick out of challenging yourself. You have abnormal touch and feel. By using the FEEL-SEE-DO process you will learn to fire the front part of your brain and thus control the ball effectively.

As a putter, you get intimately familiar with the club. Feel the grip as well as the head. As explained in Chapter 3, test the sweet spot on the putter by gently holding the putter high in the air with one hand, and with the other take a metal object like a coin or car key and poke it at different places along the face of the putter. You will feel the putter twist and turn in your outstretched hand when you strike the putter head outside the sweet spot. When you hit the sweet spot, the putter will feel solid, and it won't twist and turn in your hand. Before putting any balls to a hole, you must first be able to strike the ball on the sweet spot every time. Hitting the ball on the sweet spot will send a feeling of confidence up through your hands and into your body. However, you want hitting the ball on the sweet spot to transfer to your subconscious. To get this feeling of successfully hitting the ball on the sweet spot, you merely tap the ball around the practice green, focusing on hitting the ball on the sweet spot. Do not try to knock the ball into a hole. Just tap the ball on the sweet spot. Being a Level 6, you will have no trouble finding the sweet spot, and you are so sensitive you will know immediately when you hit the ball on the sweet spot. Furthermore, you will get the knack of hitting the ball on the sweet spot within ten to fifteen minutes of concentrated practice.

As you get better and you feel what it is like to hit the ball on the sweet spot, begin to hit the ball harder until you are hitting it twenty to thirty feet. Now begin to lag the ball to a ten-foot line, but before striking the ball, mentally FEEL what it is like. SEE the ball come close to the lag line, experience the tingle, then DO strike the ball. As you gain confidence, now place six balls in a circle three feet from the hole. As you putt, pile the balls up into the hole until it overflows. As the cup fills up and as it begins to overflow, you will become more excited, and you can't wait to do it again. At this point, you are controlling the subconscious. FEEL-SEE-DO. FEEL the sweet spot. SEE the ball go into the hole. Hear it plunk to the bottom of the cup. Feel the tingle and DO stroke one ball. Repeat the process until all six balls are putted. As you practice, always use six balls, and always put them in a circle around the cup. As you improve, increase the distance in six-inch increments. Most Level 6 golfers don't need music to help them. However, if you feel it might help use a Walkman rather than a Boom box.

It will take you a little longer to experience success, but your putting will become masterful within a reasonable period of time. The important thing is not to rush it. You have the mental makeup to be a masterful putter because the skill of putting is mostly feel and touch. Let the conscious tell the subconscious what to do through the FEEL-SEE-DO process. For you, putting is feel and touch AND THE REST IS 98 PERCENT MENTAL.

Rear Brain Dominant, Level 7, Cognitive

Your strength lies in your internal motivation, healthy sense of balance, and joy of capturing the moment. When you get focused on a singular issue, you "will" it to happen. You "will" it to happen by getting into the flow or zone. Mihaly Csikszentmihalyi has helped us understand the flow through his ideas about "The psychology of optimal experience." The flow is a state of mind in which people get so involved that nothing else matters. The experience is so joyful that they will continue in the activity over and over again even at great effort and/or sacrifice. When in the flow it is effortless, like being carried by a current. The goals are crystal clear and the feedback is constant and constructive.

While experiencing the flow the activity is absorbing, interesting, and fun. A mountain climber needs a goal of getting to the top. But the goal of getting to the top is nothing more than an excuse to climb. If there is no joy in climbing, then it is a wasted activity. The process is more important than the goal, although it is important to attain the goal. While in the flow, you transcend time and space. You get so caught up in the activity you lose track of time, and you forget where you are. Yet, you are aware of every single thing about you. The key to controlling the firing of the rear part of the brain is to consciously slip into the zone and let the subconscious take over. By using the BIRDMAN process, you will learn how to slip into the zone.

The BIRDMAN process was developed after watching Larry Bird, the legendary basketball player or the Boston Celtics, rapidly shoot three-point shots during the annual three-point shot contest. Each year he would appear to get into a zone and experience such joy, one might identify it as ecstasy. He was focused; his shooting was effortless; he had exceptional concentration; and the balls kept going through the basket. As one watched more closely, it was noticed he would shoot one ball, but before it reached the basket, he would be releasing another ball as the previous ball just reach the rim. Most of the time, as he shot balls moving around the three-point arc, two balls were always in the air. Upon closer observation, it appeared he didn't look at the basket but was focused about four to five feet from his extended shooting hand, as if he had a point or spot for the ball to cross. The point or spot was akin to the sight at the end of a barrel on a rifle, except the sight and the barrel were both imaginary. Apparently he had a sense of where he was in relationship to the basket and caught the basket in his peripheral vision while focusing on the imaginary sight four to five feet from his extended shooting hand.

As a putter, to use the BIRDMAN process you imagine the sight on the barrel to be six to ten inches from the ball rather than from the hole. As a Level 7, you will not need to use ball markers to guide you. You will intuitively see the sight. When you see the sight, you will see the line, when you see the line you will get excited. After you get excited, strike the ball.

The game of golf lends itself to more Level 7 stuff. Most golfers experience the zone from time to time. When you are in the zone, you cause things to happen; you "will" it; you can't miss. At other times, you are completely out of it. As a Level 7, you can enhance the feeling of ecstasy and increase your control of the zone by never putting the ball from the same distance when practicing. The reason you change distances every time is because when you play golf for real you don't have a practice shot first to get the feel and direction of the green. The feel and direction must be generated mentally. In the zone, you don't need practice shots; you mentally have a sense of everything. As a Level 7, on the practice green, every time you putt the ball the same distance from the hole you are consciously telling the subconscious you need to hit a practice ball first to get the feeling and direction before you hit for real. When you play for real and you can't test the green with a trial putt, you have consciously telegraphed to the subconscious you can't do it. In other words, you think when you putt balls the same distance from the hole you are gaining confidence. The truth is with Level 7s you are telling your subconscious you need a crutch. For Level 7s only, your confidence is lowered in direct proportion to the number of putts you roll the same distance from the hole. Let's say you are five feet from the hole, and in practice you hit ten balls from the same exact spot. You miss the first two, make one, miss three, and make the last four.

You leave the green satisfied and falsely confident. Now you play for real, and you end up on the real green in about the same spot. I ask you, how confident are you now? On the practice green you have successfully knocked the ball in the hole half the time. Now, for real, do you think you have a 50 percent chance of making it? Of course not. Your subconscious has taken control and is telegraphing to you loud and clear, you are no good without a couple of practice rolls; there is no way you can get the ball in the hole the first time. During practice you have programmed your mind for failure unless you can take a couple of practice shots first.

In addition to not putting the same distance from the cup, you can enhance your feeling of ecstasy and increase your control of getting in the zone by never putting with the same putter twice. Take three or four putters to the practice green with you. Alternate putters every shot and never putt the ball from the same distance twice. As you use the BIRDMAN process, you will consciously telegraph to your subconscious that you are more important than the putter. You can "will" the ball in the hole. While in the zone, you cause the future through post-living. Post-living is nothing more than you see the sight, then the line, then the ball going into the cup at which time you get excited because you have lived the future. Now all you need to do is to stroke the ball.

Determining the Power of PeopleWise® Putting

To determine the effectiveness of PeopleWise® Putting, you first record the success rate of your regular putting skill. This provides a baseline from which future progress can be measured. Find a level area on the practice putting green and mark a ten-foot distance in one-foot intervals by placing a tee each foot from the hole about three to four inches on the far side of the aimline. Putt five balls at each of the distances and calculate the percentage of successful putts made. Record the percentage in graph form using a similar format to that shown in Figure 8.1. Repeat this process and record the results for five to six sessions. This baseline information determines your skill level before becoming a PeopleWise® putter.

After you master the basics of head still, sweet spot, putter head square and the pendulum swing on the aimline path, you assess the accuracy of your putting by recording five to six sessions as you did during baseline. Be sure to only begin assessing your skill level of mastering the basics when you can execute the basics without consciously thinking. At this point, you will be putting at the percentage of the pros. Your accuracy will be around 60 percent (one foot, 100%; two feet, 100%; three feet, 95%; four feet, 70%; five feet, 60%; six feet, 50%; seven feet, 40%; eight feet, 35%; nine feet, 25%; ten feet, 20%; at total average of 59.5%). You are a good putter.

Now that you have mastered the mechanics of putting, you work on the nine steps of convincing yourself you are a masterful putter. Engage in self-talk (talk, picture, emotion) ten seconds at a time, three times a day. You must believe it because if you allow just a crack of doubt enter your subconscious it won't work. If you believe you are not a good putter, you won't be. That is a fact. The beauty about the mental part is that the subconscious believes what it is told; the tough part is keeping it up day in and day out.

After just five days of honest and convincing self-talk, you are ready to assess your skill level. After five days, begin your assessment of how well you have mastered the mental part of the game by recording five to six sessions as you did during baseline and basics. You will see a small, five-percent jump in your putting accuracy. You are a *real* good putter.

At this point you are ready to become a PeopleWise® putter by determining the location and intensity of your own brain activation. Complete the PeopleWise® Self-Assessment System found in Chapter 9, Your Brain. After determining the location and intensity of the activation of your own brain carefully, read and study your PeopleWise® Pattern Description. Take the information in your PeopleWise® Pattern Description and begin to control your subconscious. As explained before, the key is to feel the emotion *before* the execution of the skill. This self-inflicted emotion helps fire the brain so confidence and Olympian focus are realized.

Because of the specificity and clarity of how to fire your own brain, you should be able to begin to measure its effectiveness in a week to ten days of minimal practice. To assess your PeopleWise® Putting skill record five to six sessions as you did during baseline, basics, and self-talk.

Your accuracy level will now exceed 75 percent, and you have attained the status of a *real, real* good putter.

To get beyond real, real good you have to practice, and that falls outside the realm of this book. However, you might want to experiment with trying to fire other parts of your brain by mastering the techniques outlined in PeopleWise® Pattern Descriptions other than your own. Since you are making the majority of your putts, your brain is firing repeatedly and sending success messages to your muscles and nervous system. Experimentation now leads to a fine tuning of brain activation where before, at less than 50 percent, the subconscious was confused, and the brain activation was scattered. Stay on the PeopleWise® Putting program and you will continue to maintain the status of being real, real good for the rest of your golf days.

When you reach the 75 percent accuracy mark, send us a completed photocopy of Figure 8.1 and we will send you an "I'm Real, Real Good" bumper sticker. Send the completed photocopy of Figure 8.1 to:

> Management & Motivation, Inc.
> c/o PeopleWise® Putting
> P O Box 215
> University, MS 38677

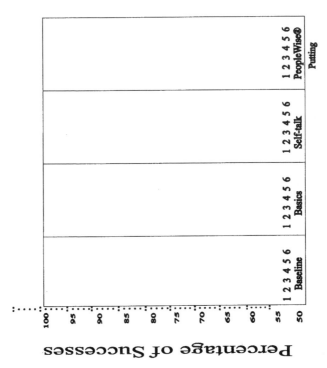

Figure 8.1. Sample Format for Recording and Graphic Percentages of Successes to Determine the Power of PeopleWise® Putting

Name:

Address:

Phone:

E-mail:

Attain the 75 percent success rate. Photocopy and complete.
Then send for your "I'm Real, Real Good" bumper sticker.

Send to: Management & Motivation, Inc.
c/o PeopleWise® Putting
P O Box 215
University, MS 38677

CHAPTER 9
Your Brain

Just exactly what is PeopleWise® Putting? PeopleWise® refers to people becoming wise about themselves and others. As mentioned in the beginning of this book, individuals who become PeopleWise® know what makes them tick and how to tick better. PeopleWise® Putting teaches what you need to know to putt better and how to do it by knowing the way you learn best.

PeopleWise® Putting begins with learning the basics followed by mastering the mental part of visual imagery and mental rehearsal and then capping off the skill development with controlling the subconscious by utilizing the latest techniques known in brain science. Brain science reveals the importance of how emotion affects the activation of brain waves. When you control the activation of your brain, you increase your confidence and you attain Olympian focus.

The following, PeopleWise® Self-Assessment System, identifies ways and means that you can use to understand your preferred Level of functioning, where your brain is most likely to activate and its intensity and subsequently exactly how you go about using this information to improve your putting.

The PeopleWise® Self-Assessment System is a paper/pencil instrument that produces a graphic depiction of where your brain has a tendency to activate and its intensity. Once the preferred brain location and activation intensity are determined, then specific suggestions on your Level of functioning and how you can improve your putting is reported in your own PeopleWise® Pattern Description.

Each PeopleWise® Pattern Description contains the following information:

Level, Number, and Name
Characteristics
Brain Activation
Basics
Mind Control
PeopleWise® Putting
Strengths
Weaknesses
Improvement
Must Read

PEOPLEWISE® SELF-ASSESSMENT SYSTEM

Following each of the twenty-one statements below are four possible choices. Select the sentence, phrase, or word that describes you best or that you prefer most. Place an X in the appropriate box. If more than one choice appeals to you, force yourself to just pick one that appeals to you and move on. Keep in mind, this is not a test. There are no right or wrong answers. You can't pass or fail. The purpose of the instrument is to give you a ballpark reading regarding your Level of functioning and where and at what intensity your brain is firing.

Put an **X** in the box of your choice. ONLY ONE **X** FOR EACH STATEMENT.

1. I FEEL IT IS IMPORTANT TO:

   ☐ A. Be steady and secure
   ☐ B. Be seen by others as important and respected
   ☐ C. Have many fine friends and acquaintances
   ☐ D. Develop and realize my full potential

2. THIS I BELIEVE ABOUT FRIENDSHIP:

   ☐ A. It is a lasting and permanent relationship
   ☐ B. It is a give and take process
   ☐ C. Without friends life is nothing
   ☐ D. Some people need friends, some people don't

3. THE WORD THAT DESCRIBES ME BEST IS:

   ☐ A. Reliable
   ☐ B. Competitive
   ☐ C. Reflective
   ☐ D. Transcending

4. I ENJOY SITUATIONS WHICH PROVIDE AN OPPORTUNITY FOR ME TO:

- ☐ A. Increase my prestige and receive well-deserved attention
- ☐ B. Develop plans and programs for my future
- ☐ C. Meet new people and make new friends
- ☐ D. Utilize talents and capabilities I don't often use

5. THIS I BELIEVE ABOUT THE AMERICAN WAY OF LIFE:

- ☐ A. McDonald's is taking over
- ☐ B. Competition has brought about highest standards of living ever achieved in history
- ☐ C. Church, Mom, apple pie, best there is
- ☐ D. Confused society with misplaced values

6. THE WORD THAT DESCRIBES ME BEST IS:

- ☐ A. Contextual
- ☐ B. Cordial
- ☐ C. Driven
- ☐ D. Consistent

7. I TEND TO PLACE THE GREATEST EMPHASIS ON:

- ☐ A. Developing self-confidence, pride, and influence over others
- ☐ B. The achievement of personal goals and objectives
- ☐ C. Building a secure life for myself and others who may be dependent on me
- ☐ D. Being with and enjoying the company of my friends

8. THIS I BELIEVE ABOUT SIN:

- ☐ A. There are no levels of sin — wrong is wrong
- ☐ B. Sin is everywhere
- ☐ C. No such thing — dreamed up to scare people
- ☐ D. Different people consider different things sin

9. THE WORD THAT DESCRIBES ME BEST IS:

- ☐ A. Entrepreneurial
- ☐ B. Dependable
- ☐ C. Childlike (not childish)
- ☐ D. Altruistic

10. FROM TIME TO TIME I THINK ABOUT:

- ☐ A. My safety and security
- ☐ B. Increasing my competence
- ☐ C. Improving myself so that I could do even more worthwhile and challenging things
- ☐ D. Getting to know people, pleasing them, and maintaining their friendship

11. THIS I BELIEVE ABOUT MARRIAGE:

- ☐ A. A state of mind, not a piece of paper
- ☐ B. A way to insure that both partners try harder to stay together
- ☐ C. Sacred union of two people who love each other and should be faithful to one another
- ☐ D. Good for some, bad for others

12. THE WORD THAT DESCRIBES ME BEST IS:

- ☐ A. Change-oriented
- ☐ B. Inventive
- ☐ C. Orthodox
- ☐ D. Amiable

13. I TEND TO LOOK FOR:

- ☐ A. Friendly people who support one another
- ☐ B. Freedom and an opportunity to grow as much as I can
- ☐ C. Recognition for outstanding performance
- ☐ D. Consistency, stability, and security

14. THIS I BELIEVE ABOUT RELIGION:

- ☐ A. It is necessary for living a full and meaningful life
- ☐ B. It is interesting and important to many people
- ☐ C. People generally need someone or something to believe in
- ☐ D. Religion is becoming too commercial

15. THE WORD THAT DESCRIBES ME BEST IS:

- ☐ A. People-oriented
- ☐ B. Industrious
- ☐ C. Totality
- ☐ D. Persistent

16. I WOULD BECOME DISCOURAGED IF:

- ☐ A. Things became mundane and I found myself doing the same things over and over again
- ☐ B. The overall conditions became unstable and depressed
- ☐ C. I started to be taken for granted and was by-passed on some promotional opportunities
- ☐ D. I ended up doing work by myself with very little opportunity to see or work with others

17. THIS I BELIEVE ABOUT OTHER PEOPLE:

- ☐ A. People are basically no good, but I love them anyway
- ☐ B. People make me feel secure
- ☐ C. People, as I see them, are beautiful, if only the world could be beautiful with all those people
- ☐ D. People are the most unique set of organisms in the world

18. THE WORD THAT DESCRIBES ME BEST IS:

- ☐ A. Companionable
- ☐ B. Loyal
- ☐ C. Adventurous
- ☐ D. Inner-directed

19. WHAT IS VERY IMPORTANT TO ME IS:

  ☐ A. Being part of a top-notch group with good fellow-ship
  ☐ B. Knowing that I am one of "the best" and being respected for it
  ☐ C. Being required to stretch a little, tackle a difficult task, and see the results
  ☐ D. Clear-cut ground rules and reasonable protection

20. THIS I BELIEVE ABOUT RULES:

  ☐ A. Too much emphasis on them
  ☐ B. Useful if reasonable
  ☐ C. I can take them or leave them, but I try to obey most of the important rules
  ☐ D. Are made to be obeyed

21. THE WORD THAT DESCRIBES ME BEST IS:

  ☐ A. Sensing
  ☐ B. Conventional
  ☐ C. Fearless
  ☐ D. Persuasive

James S. Payne and Larry W. Wagster

ANALYSIS FOR PEOPLEWISE®
SELF-ASSESSMENT SYSTEM

INSTRUCTIONS: Place your choices with an **X** alongside the alternatives (A, B, C, or D) in the space below. Work across the sheet for each of the twenty-one statements. Remember, you will have three blanks for each statement. Then add the **X**'s in each column to obtain your Totals.

1A ____	1B ____	1C ____	1D ____
2A ____	2B ____	2C ____	2D ____
3A ____	3B ____	3C ____	3D ____
4B ____	4A ____	4C ____	4D ____
5C ____	5B ____	5D ____	5A ____
6D ____	6C ____	6B ____	6A ____
7C ____	7A ____	7D ____	7B ____
8A ____	8B ____	8C ____	8D ____
9B ____	9A ____	9D ____	9C ____
10A ____	10B ____	10D ____	10C ____
11C ____	11B ____	11A ____	11D ____
12C ____	12A ____	12D ____	12B ____
13D ____	13C ____	13A ____	13B ____
14A ____	14C ____	14D ____	14B ____
15D ____	15B ____	15A ____	15C ____
16B ____	16C ____	16D ____	16A ____
17B ____	17D ____	17C ____	17A ____
18B ____	18C ____	18A ____	18D ____
19D ____	19B ____	19A ____	19C ____
20D ____	20B ____	20A ____	20C ____
21B ____	21D ____	21A ____	21C ____

TOTAL [ ]	[ ]	[ ]	[ ]
LEVEL [4]	[5]	[6]	[7]
LOCATION [LEFT]	[RIGHT]	[FRONT]	[REAR]

To chart your brain activation and intensity, take your totals from the previous analysis and block in (use pencil or pen) the number of cells for each Level in the Brain Activation Graphic (Figure 9.2). For clarity, block in the cells as indicated by the numbers within the cells. For example, TOTAL: 13 LEVEL 4 LEFT, 3 LEVEL 5 RIGHT, 4 LEVEL 6 FRONT, 1 LEVEL 7 REAR (See Figure 9.1 below). This person is predominately functioning at Level 4 and firing in the left hemisphere.

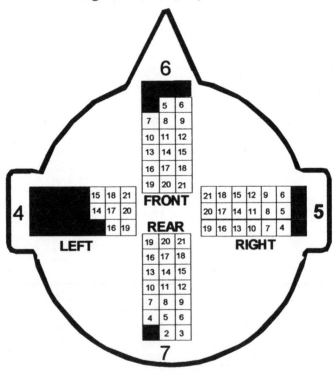

Figure 9.1: Example of Brain Activation Graphic

(13 LEVEL 4 LEFT, 3 LEVEL 5 RIGHT,
4 LEVEL 6 FRONT, 1 LEVEL 7 REAR)
This individual would be considered a Level 4 left brainer.

PeopleWise® Self-Assessment System
Brain Activation Graphic

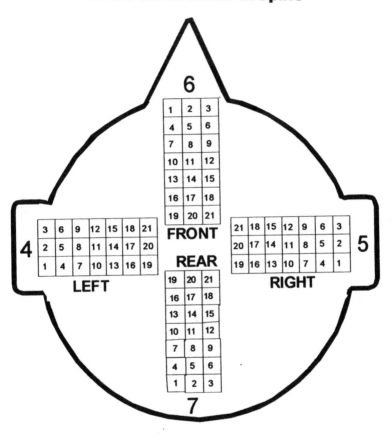

Figure 9.2: Brain Activation Graphic.

Block in the number of cells for each level.

Use your totals from the Analysis for
PeopleWise® Self-Assessment System.

For a ballpark interpretation of your results, study your completed Brain Activation Graphic. The following section, PeopleWise® Pattern Descriptions, contains four basic Levels and six Blends. If the bulk of your scores fall in a particular Level or area, turn to an explanation of that Level. If you are a combination of Levels, where the two most scored Levels are five or less points from one another, then turn to the appropriate Blend. A spread of greater than five points yields to the Level with the greatest score. The basic patterns included are:

> LEVELS: 4, 5, 6, 7
> BLENDS: 4-5, 5-6, 4-6, 4-7, 5-7, 6-7

For persons interested in greater precision in determining the location and intensity of brain activation, the **PeopleWise® Profile System** is available. The **PeopleWise® Profile System** is more sophisticated and has more options. For more information on the **PeopleWise® Profile System**, call or write for a free brochure and catalog:

> Management & Motivation, Inc.
> c/o PeopleWise® Profile System
> P O Box 215
> University, MS 38677
> 1-800-514-7626
> mm@watervalley.net
> www.managementandmotivation.com
> FAX#: (662) 281-8780

PeopleWise® Pattern Descriptions
LEVEL 4, ABSOLUTIST

Characteristics

You are driven by principle. You have high standards and high expectations for yourself and others. You will sacrifice for those things you believe are important. You work hard, and some may believe you work too hard. If you agree to do it, you do it. You have a tenacity that you believe is focused while others may see you as dogged. You are steady and can be counted on. You don't seek recognition but expect to be treated fairly. You are undemonstrative, but if pushed, can show anger or at least hold your ground and be firm. You are sensitive to manipulation and may occasionally wonder what people are up to or what they want. You want to know what is expected of you, how you will be evaluated, what the goals are, and what the time lines are. You work best in a predictable environment, and you will shoulder more than you share without complaint. When the going gets tough, the tough get going. You are not hesitant to put your shoulder to the wheel or put your nose to the grindstone. You are a meat and potatoes type of no-frills person. You can put off until tomorrow and save for a rainy day.

Brain Activation

Your brain activates predominately in the left hemisphere. Your skill improves under a regimen or system that moves from Step 1, to Step 2, to Step 3, etc. You are good at following guidelines, and you feel comfortable with principles that help with improved skill development. You can benefit from watching an expert whom you respect and admire. Your skill improves by periodically reminding yourself to go back to the basics. Review your stance, head placement, and position of arms. The object is to get your complex body to do the same movement, time and time again. In your case, practice does make perfect, providing you stick to the basics. Don't over think and don't over analyze your movement. Just repeat your movement exactly as it should be done again and again and again. See yourself doing it right. Visualize yourself doing it exactly as it is to be done. Become mentally tough. Work your mind as hard as you work your body. You can benefit from some muscle-memory training that teaches you how to perfect your movement through modeling a perfect motion. One of the most effective ways to utilize muscle memory training is to study a video, DVD, or compact disc of a professional executing the desired skill and then you physically repeating the movement over and over.

Basics

As a Level 4, left brainer, you will grip the club a little firmer than usual. Thus hitting the ball exactly on the sweet spot isn't all that important. The important thing is don't grip the club so firm it causes muscle tension in your shoulders or arms. You putt best when you are mechanical. Don't try to hold the club loose and don't get fancy with your stroke. Keep it basic and simple. Hold the club and stroke it similar to how you shake hands — firm with purpose.

You will have a good sense of direction of the putt, but distance will be an area you need to constantly work on. You will try to hit longer putts with more force — don't. Practice on swinging the putter on the same arc with the same speed. When you need more distance increase the length of the arc. As you practice, note how far the ball goes from a four-inch back swing compared to a six-inch back swing. You will quickly realize you can judge distances by how far you move the club on the back swing. Remember, the back swing is the same distance as the follow through.

Your left brain will help you keep your head still, putter square and your swing on the aimline path. These basics will come naturally with very little practice although occasionally you will need to remind yourself to stick to the basics.

Your main problem will be distance. Control distance with mathematics — at a four-inch back swing it goes so far, at a six, at eight, etc. With very little practice you will experience an insight regarding distance, but distance is what you need to work on every time you hit a couple of balls on the practice green.

Select a putter that you feel comfortable with. You will know it when you find it. The putter you select will be you and it will become a valuable part of you. Give your putter a name and never divorce or cheat on your putter. Be loyal to it and it will be loyal to you. Don't even think about trying a long handled putter. For you, a long handled putter is a mismatch, and it ain't a good marriage to a Level 4 brain.

Mind Control

You are mentally tough. You have a strong will. In order to get the creative subconscious to help you, your picture must be very clear. This will be hard for you because for you, mental toughness means stick-to-itive-ness, grinding it out, and persevering. Playing mental games does not come natural to you, so picture yourself as a perfectly constructed robot. See yourself as a robot that addresses the ball the same way exactly every time, head just behind the ball, kept still, pendulum swing like a Grandfather clock, tick-tock.

See yourself sinking putt after putt — tick-tock, tick-tock. See yourself sinking putts at varying distances with the same tick-tock movement except with varying lengths in the arc. As you see yourself sinking putt after putt, talk to yourself about how great you are and how steady you are and how repeatable your stroke is. And finally, the most important thing is to build up excitement as you mentally keep sinking putts. Do this three times a day. Because you are so methodical try doing your visualization while driving to and from work or while watching a commercial on television. Visualization and mental rehearsal will not be easy for you but keep reminding yourself of the power of brain washing techniques used on POWs. Brainwashing is discussed in Chapter 6, Mind Control, under Step six.

When you do this for twenty to thirty days, it will become a habit and you will automatically continue to do it not only for putting but also for other things that are important in your life.

Keep reminding yourself to review the basics.

PeopleWise® Putting

Once you have mastered the basics without consciously thinking and your visualization of yourself as the perfect robot is imbedded in your head, you are ready to control the firing of the subconscious through a SEE-DO process.

Review the SEE-DO process as described in Chapter 8, PeopleWise® Putting. Keep these thoughts in mind. SEE — you mentally see the ball go into the hole and hear the plunk as it drops in the cup, which sends excitement throughout your entire body. After feeling the excitement you DO — by striking the ball. Remember; strike the ball after you feel the excitement. This will be a little difficult in the beginning because you are not an emotional being but once you actually do it a few times in succession you will catch the power of your own brain and it will become automatic — *hit the ball after the emotion.*

If you ever catch yourself talking to yourself while putting, go back to the basics then to mind control and then to PeopleWise® Putting. Don't try to experiment with your stroke or your mind. Your strength is in your repetition. Do the SEE-DO approach as described in Chapter 8 ,and continue to work on distance.

Strengths

Things done right; reliable; high standards; self-discipline; good follow through/follow up

Weaknesses

Sometimes over-opinionated; suspicious; worrisome; at times over does it; resistant to change

Improvement

Be more flexible; share with others more; become more visionary; try out new things; take calculated risks

Must Read

Armour, T. (1953). *How to play our best golf all the time.*
New York: Simon and Schuster.

Armour, T. (1967). *Tommy Armour's ABC's of golf.* New York: Simon and Schuster.

Both of these classic books have short sections devoted to putting. For the Level 4 brain, they are refreshing and insightful. Both books in their entirety will be of great benefit to any left-brained player.

Morrice, P. (2000). *The golf magazine putting handbook.*
New York: The Lyons Press.

A comprehensive book on putting with accurate instruction that is succinct and focused. An excellent book for a Level 4 mind.

PeopleWise® Pattern Descriptions
LEVEL 5, MATERIALIST

Characteristics

You are competitive. You have high energy. You like to win and you challenge yourself. You have an internal desire that pushes you to exceed. You have unusual bursts of energy. You don't need much sleep. You enjoy life and consider yourself zestful. You express yourself openly and some consider you animated or possibly outspoken. You are spirited and very active. You like to do a variety of things and are spontaneous. You search for new and different ways to do things. You like change. Although you can set goals, you find oftentimes you exceed your expectations and end up in places and situations you hadn't planned for. You like yourself and are confident. You will take a calculated risk and you learn from your mistakes. You don't look back. You are a no-nonsense person and want to get on with it. You don't like to waste time, yet you enjoy time. You work hard but more importantly, you work smart. You like to think things out and occasionally scribble random isolated ideas down on paper. When the going gets tough, you get competitive. You stand tall and walk with authority. You project enthusiasm. You plan for tomorrow but believe tomorrow is now.

Brain Activation

Your brain activates predominately in the right hemisphere. Your skill improves with study, calculation, and analysis. For you, practice does not make perfect. For you, perfect practice makes perfect. Your time is valuable; therefore, your practice must be focused and intense. You are a cause-and-effect person. You believe you can cause things to happen. You like to act on the environment.

The important thing is not doing it exactly right. The important thing is doing it with maximum effort and, or course, accomplishing the goal. For you, desire is more important than basics. The body is complex, and the job is to achieve, even when your body is out of sync. You do this by mind over matter, visualizing what you want to accomplish, were the ball is to go, the end result. This type of visualization will help you achieve and excel. You can't over analyze or over think. You are a cognitive being. Going back to basics is a waste of time for you and is boring. Do not try to visualize your movement. You must project out and visualize what is to happen rather than how it is to be done. You can greatly benefit from practicing visual imagery and mental rehearsal; your skill level will take a quantum leap forward.

Basics

As a Level 5, right brainer, your skill in putting goes beyond the basics. You are not regimented or mechanical. You are calculative and cognitive. You realize each day you get up a different person. Some days your body is more fluid than others. Sometimes you are more alive, alert and quick. You believe your job is not to get your complex body and nervous system to do the same thing over and over but you believe you take your complex body and nervous system and use it to just get the ball in the hole regardless of how you feel.

Head still, sweet spot and smooth pendulum swing are guidelines, not absolutes. Perfecting mechanics will only make your swing more jerky. It is more important to get the ball in the hole than study how to get it in the hole. Even though you are goal directed, you benefit from knowing every thing you can. Nevertheless, the bottom line is winning, having a personal best, and scoring well. While scoring well, it is important to look like a pro. Look like you know what you are doing. Look good.

Keeping all this in mind, you will try new things and experiment with new ideas. You will take a risk. You decide what is best based on how well it works. You like theory, strategy, and processes that attain results. You are an excellent candidate for the long-handled putter if it only looked better. Take the information on determining the power of PeopleWise® Putting found at the end of Chapter 8. Get a long-handled putter; read how to use it and why it is superior. Practice with it until it feels somewhat natural and then test it against your regular putter. Find a level area on the practice putting green and mark a ten-foot distance in one-foot intervals by placing a tee each foot from the hole. Putt five balls at each of the one-foot distances and calculate your scores using the long-handled putter and your regular putter. Do this for five or six sessions and don't be surprised if the long-handled putter wins but still doesn't look pretty. In order for you to choose a long-handled putter over the traditional putter, you must convince yourself it is superior. This can only be done through objective measurement. Even with objective measurement it still doesn't look good in your bag. For you to use it, it will have to be real superior not just a little bit better.

Why do you putt better with a long-handled putter? Because you are intelligent and well coordinated, and the long-handled putter gives you greater control of the putter head with a simplified putting stroke. By the way, Level 4, left-brained putters score better with traditional putters and Level 5, right-brained putters score better with long-handled putters. The reason for the difference is because Level 4 putters rely on mechanics, but you, as a Level 5, rely on cognition.

Even with all this, you will have a tendency to go back to the traditional putter. If you go back to the traditional putter, just use the basics of head still, sweet spot, and pendulum swing as guidelines, and move on to mastering mind control through visual imagery and mental rehearsal.

Going back to basics will never help you but a long-handled putter will. Regardless of your decision, your strength in putting lies between your ears.

Mind Control

All you need to do is to reread Chapter 6, Mind Control. After studying this chapter you will know exactly what to do. Crafting a picture of you being a putting master and envisioning superior performance on the putting green will be your forté.

Self-talk (using talk, picture, emotion) will be perfected within a day or two. Your problem will be overconfidence and overemotion when failure is experienced. You must channel your explosiveness into positiveness by being reasonable and forgiving. Don't try to minimize your emotion. Just take charge and direct it.

Don't be tempted to picture the perfect stroke and praise yourself on form and function because your psyche knows the result is what matters. Picture yourself sinking putts; mentally see, hear, and smell success.

When you fail, remember one flush, one reprimand is enough, then back to ball in hole — ball in hole — ball in hole.

In Chapter 6 Mind Control under the ninth step, Measure the Outcome — Feedback, you may want to break the putting stroke down into smaller units. For instance you could count the percentage of time you kept your head still without watching the ball if you were having trouble with this aspect of the stroke. But you must also calculate the total putts used and compare it over time. You are data driven and results oriented. Play to that strength. Also keep in mind violating small segments of the mechanics is not that important to you. Your subconscious is so strong you will make putts with minor flaws in your mechanics.

Even though you don't need help crafting your picture, you might visualize yourself being a brain surgeon with your putter being an instrument of fine precision and the putting green as your operating table.

PeopleWise® Putting

Once you get the mechanics down as best you can by realizing they are guidelines, or better yet by adopting the use of a long-handled putter, and you should curb your confidence level into a realistic picture coupled with continuous measurement and feedback. Then you are ready to blow your socks off by becoming a PeopleWise® Putter using the TUBE technique.

Study the TUBE process found in Chapter 8, PeopleWise® Putting. Putting the ball into the imaginary tube tricks the subconscious into thinking the cup is closer than it is. The danger is, this works so fast and it is so easy you will think the secret is in seeing the tube as opposed to feeling the emotion before striking the ball. Remember, you imagine the ball going through the tube; you hear the imaginary plunk which makes you actually tingle with excitement; then you stroke the ball. You must condition yourself to feel the excitement first before striking the ball.

If you forget what it is like to feel the excitement, move the ball back ten feet before hitting some balls toward the cup. Every time one falls in, you will experience the excitement. The excitement is what you must condition yourself to feel before you strike the ball. The excitement fires the right side of your brain. You must mentally make it fire rather than letting the ball going into the cup fire the brain.

As mentioned before, when you fail only flush once with a reprimand or if you put a reasonable stroke on the ball blame the grass or green. You are smarter than your subconscious. Now you know how to control the subconscious by using the TUBE technique.

Strengths

Focus; high energy; calculated risks; attainment of goals; achievement

Weaknesses

Impulsive; erratic; impatient; outspoken; at times, too self-congratulatory

Improvement

Listen more; slow down; schedule time for self; write to your mother; take time to smell the roses.

Must Read

Pelz, D. (2000). *Dave Pelz's putting bible*. New York: Doubleday.

You will be a better putter after reading this book; I guarantee it even if Dave Pelz doesn't. Your right side of the brain will eat the words right off the page. This book is perfect for you to develop a repeatable stroke that is precise. If you can afford one of his clinics, it will change your putting and life forever.

PeopleWise® Pattern Descriptions
LEVEL 6, SOCIOCENTRIC

Characteristics

You are a people person. You have a sensitivity that is exceptional. You are an excellent listener, and people enjoy being in your presence. You don't just listen, you get involved in the situation, and others can sense you are engaged with them. Your body language and eye contact express honesty, sensitivity, concern, and deep feeling. You are a giver, an unconditional giver who expects nothing in return. However, if someone pays you back for the kindnesses you unselfishly bestowed, you will humbly, almost embarrassingly, accept, but deep down you wish they had not reciprocated. You have a hypersensitivity to how people feel — happy/sad, excited/depressed, joyful/angry, and apathetic/concerned. Regardless of the situation, you remain optimistic, positive, and most importantly, hopeful. You are not goal-driven, you are purpose-driven. You take time to smell the roses. When the going gets tough, the tough get sensitive. You are not so much interested in the past or the future, but focus on the present — what is happening to us now, what we are feeling, what is really going on between us at this moment in time. Spontaneity, creativity, and expression of self are key to your very being.

Brain Activation

Your brain activates predominately in the front. Your skill improves when you feel the process or you get into your rhythm. One of the difficulties regarding skill improvement is directly related to you not wanting to beat another person or win at the expense of the other person losing. Therefore, you are not competitively motivated to improve. You are not driven to win.

What is important to you is, did you have fun, did you do your best, did you work as a team, and did you learn. One way to help you improve a skill is to measure your improvement against yourself. As you become more skilled, you gain an appreciation for yourself, not because you can beat anyone, but because you see yourself getting better.

Once you have mastered the basics, you will find you are a natural for studying psycho cybernetics. This basic type of visual imaging and mental rehearsal benefits you because it relies on feeling the success before it happens. You feel the success by visualizing the outcome of the skill before execution. Once you feel the thrill by mentally seeing the outcome, you are in a position to increase your concentration, focus, and confidence. It is unlikely your skill will improve with a step-by-step regimented program or an intense study of the skill through calculation and analysis. For you, practice doesn't make perfect, nor does perfect practice make perfect. For you, mentally practicing, visualizing, feeling the rhythm is as important as actually physically practicing once you have mastered the basics. Anything you can do to heighten the feeling of success will enhance your skill. Your key is awareness, sensitivity, and feeling.

Basics

As a Level 6, front brainer, your skill in putting lies in touch, feel, sensitivity, and rhythm. You are not the type of person who will force yourself to do regimented basics, but you realize the importance of fundamentals. To master the basics you need only to know what they are and then while executing the skill focus your attention on the specific fundamental you want to master. For instance, if you want to keep your head still, do not try to hold your head still. Instead, focus on what your head does while you stroke the ball. Using this awareness technique you will self-correct without consciously forcing your head not to move.

To gain rhythm, begin with a tick-tock approach. As you move the clubhead back say to yourself "tick" and as the clubhead strikes the ball say "tock." Without hitting a ball just move the club back and forth in a pendulum motion saying "tick-tock, tick-tock, tick-tock." This will help you establish a good rhythm.

The basics of head still, sweet spot, putterhead square and swing on the aimline path can all be mastered using the awareness technique. The tick-tock technique will help get you into good rhythm. Review Chapter 3, Nuts and Bolts, and pay particular attention when the awareness technique is described.

A traditional putter is best because a long-handled putter restricts your natural freedom of movement. Try choking down on the putter four to six inches. For a Level 6, choking down on the club provides a looseness in the arms and shoulders that enhances rhythm and freedom of the stroke. If choking down on the club makes you feel more relaxed and loose, then actually cut off part of the handle of the club and have it re-gripped. The key to the basics is becoming so aware of the club that it becomes an extension of your body, and when the ball hits the sweet spot, it feels like it was tapped with the tip of your finger. The putter is nothing more than an extended finger.

Mind Control

When using mind control, you visualize the movement and feel the rhythm and do not focus on results. You are not a result person. If the ball goes in, fine; if it doesn't, fine. The important thing is to know what you can control. You can control your stroke but you can only influence the ball. On any green at any time the ball may have a mind of its own.

Your picture is focused on technique and style. Self-talk (using talk, picture, emotion) will emphasize the emotion. You control the emotion by bringing it into the present. How do you feel now, and how do you control it now? This nowness is as important as it gets. Your visual imagery and mental rehearsal must be so attuned to the now that you increase your sensitivity to a level of hypersensitivity. At this level, the creative subconscious has a clear target, and you will maximize the power of your subconscious. Stay in the present. "The past is history, the future's a mystery. Being alive in this moment is a gift — that's why they call it the present" (Parent, 2002, p. 90).

PeopleWise® Putting

After mastering the basics through heightened awareness and conquering mind control through visual imagery and mental rehearsal that is present moment attuned, you are ready to control the firing of the front part of your brain through the FEEL-SEE-DO process.

Look over the FEEL-SEE-DO process outlined in Chapter 8. It will take you longer to improve your putting because you must learn to trust and believe in yourself. Trust can not be rushed. Trust is built in small increments, not big jumps or leaps.

First you FEEL. The FEEL is gradually developed throughout the sequence of mastering the art of putting. You gain FEEL during basic training through awareness. You enhance FEEL with mind control by becoming present moment sensitive. As you begin to take control of assisting the front part of your brain to activate, you de-emphasize results and focus entirely on getting so familiar with the putter it becomes a part of your body just as a walking/mobility cane becomes part of a blind person's life. Do not try to name your putter because that would be like assigning a name to one of your fingers or to your hand. The putter is you and not an inanimate object.

Getting the FEEL is a process that you continuously perfect. Next you SEE. You mentally see the ball go into the cup, hear it plunk, and feel the tingle of excitement. This excitement must burst into a present moment feeling that leads to DO. You strike the putt.

Keep in mind, be patient. It will take you longer to show improvement, but you have the DNA to excel in putting. Most people agree putting is feel and touch, and feel and touch play to your strengths.

Strengths

Sensitivity; purposeful intentions; caring; sharing team player.

Weaknesses

Can't say no; others control time; appear to lack direction; will settle for less; indecisive at times.

Improvement

Set personal goals; learn to tactfully say no; become proactive; spend time with people not like you; master a physical skill.

Must Read

Gallwey, W. T. (1990). *The inner game of golf*. New York: Random House.

If there ever was a book written for the front-brain thinker this is it. This book is very well written with oodles of specific awareness techniques, practices and drills that will immediately improve any Level 6 putter.

James S. Payne and Larry W. Wagster

PeopleWise® Pattern Descriptions
LEVEL 7, COGNITIVE

Characteristics

You hold yourself in high esteem and see yourself as principle-centered, internally motivated, and destined to make things happen that contribute to the greater good. You are intrigued with existence itself and enjoy living life to its fullest. You are complex and live multiple lives. You need little sleep, and your mind is always running at full speed. You never get depressed, but sometimes you get confused, especially when you witness injustices. However, you seek clarity through meditation and/or solitude, and you are back on track before you know it. You enjoy ambiguity, variety, differences, and occasionally chaos. You view the world contextually. Thus, you can handle, value, and appreciate extreme differences in opinions and life styles. You have conquered fear. You have either had a brush with death or intimately know of someone who has. You have no fear of boss, survival, social acceptance, political pressure, economic strife, or death. You are autonomous, inner-directed, and are cognizantly complex. You work on many things at once, yet you are focused on each multi-task. On occasion, you can get so focused on a singular issue you actually "will" it to happen. You think and behave so differently from the masses that your close friends admire you and have extremely high regard for you. Your enemies fear you and are confused by your activities. Many outsiders see you as unique, odd, different, and/or possibly crazy. The world is a better place because of you. You are not interested in the past, present, or future. You are interested in process. While others ponder if there is life after death, you wonder if there is life after birth.

Brain Activation

Your brain activates predominately in the rear. When you want, your skill level may become Olympian; however, since you are more interested in processes and experiences than you are in outcomes, you may excel in spurts, just to see if you can do it. You love to test limits, and you like to do things out of the ordinary: balloon, mountain climb, juggle, etc. You can master the basics of most any skill in much less time than most people, and you understand the value of focus, concentration, and confidence. True skill excellence will be achieved by trying it in an entirely different way than it has been done before. If you select a skill that intrigues you and you stay with it for a significant period of time, you will excel. How can you get yourself to stay with something for a significant period of time? No one knows, but experience and observation suggest that the skill must fascinate you to the point you will test the existing limits, time and time again. The best advice is to look for answers outside the skill itself, but, of course, you already know that.

Basics

As a Level 7 rear brainer, your skill in putting lies in you getting in the zone or flow. For you the basics are to be experimented with, tested, and played with. For you, the basics change as you get new information about you, your putter, the ball, the green, and the situation. You will not jump randomly from idea to idea but you will experience insights, paradigm shifts, and breakthroughs.

Levels 4, 5, and 6 benefit by placing their head just behind the ball and keeping it still while stroking the ball. Your head placement and movement, or lack of movement, are to be experimented with. For instance, if you haven't already tried it, you will eventually focus on the hole while putting rather than looking at the ball. Only you can decide what is best. Some Level 7 putters hit the ball way out on the toe of the putter head explaining it gives them heightened feeling and sensitivity. You will experiment with putting English on the ball by swinging off the aimline path or holding your putterhead slightly diagonal to the aimline. For you, basics are situational not absolutes nor guidelines. Nothing is sacred or axiomatic.

For periods of time you will adopt your own unique stance and procedure for putting. This will be your foundation from which you will exercise your real strength, which is mental. The key is to blend the mental with the physical. Getting at one with yourself and the process of stroking the putt is your ultimate goal.

Mind Control

For Level 7 brains, mind control goes to a slightly different level than the purported self-talk using talk, picture, emotion found in Chapter 6, Mind Control. Level 7 brains border on daydreaming and fanaticizing. The picture formed for the creative subconscious to hone in on is actually "lived" in the brain. It is imbedded in the head. At times, it is difficult for the Level 7 to distinguish reality from mental imagery. In extreme cases, the mental imagery is reality or it becomes a reality.

In Chapter 6, Mind Control, the nine steps are designed to help an individual gain confidence and visualize as being a masterful putter. If people see themselves as not being skilled at putting, then no matter how well they master the mechanics they will not putt well. Confidence is knowing you are going to be successful before you execute the task. The Level 7 brain knows they are good, skilled, masterful… They are not overly confident nor falsely confident. They really are not confident at all. They just know they are good. They know they are good without ever striking the ball. The key to mind control is getting them to strike the ball.

Once they begin to actually strike the ball the next step is to get them intrigued and fascinated in putting. Once intrigued and fascinated, they will focus on perfecting their putting skill. Here is the problem; this book shows you how to get real, real good with little practice. When the Level 7 becomes focused, they become enveloped in the task. They become absorbed to the point of being addicted to the task. They practice and experiment tirelessly. The Level 7 loves practice, which goes beyond the scope of this book. Since the Level 7 doesn't get depressed and doesn't need much sleep, the task becomes them. They become one with themselves and the task. What PeopleWise® Putting offers are some ideas and suggestions on things and ways to try that the Level 7 brain may find worthy of their effort.

PeopleWise® Putting

Abraham Maslow, the eminent psychologist and scholar writes about the Japanese-Zen based word *muga*. A *muga* is a present-moment, peak experience. It is a time when one experiences something wholeheartedly. It is a time when individuals become so absorbed in the event they transcend time and space. Transcending time and space means during this absorption people lose track of time and don't consciously know where they are. Most everyone has experienced a muga at some time in his or her life. *Mugas* are sometimes experienced while engaged in a sporting event like tennis, skiing, deep-sea diving, or jogging. Individuals get so wrapped up in the activity they don't know where they are or what time it is. *Mugas* can be experienced while reading when the reader begins to enter the book or live the story they are reading about. The Japanese experience a muga while drinking tea — they really don't drink the tea they experience the joy of the event while drinking the tea.

Mihaly Csikszentmihalyi, the contemporary scholar on the workings of the mind has helped clarify the *muga* state of being by explaining what happens when a person gets into the zone or flow. The flow is defined as an optimal experience. It is a state of mind in which people get so involved that nothing else matters. As explained in Chapter 8, PeopleWise® Putting, in the section Rear Brain Dominant, Level 7, Cognitive, the experience is so joyful that the person will continue the activity over and over again at great effort and/or sacrifice. When in the flow, it is effortless, like being carried by a current.

Level 7 brains can get into the flow at will. Other Levels only experience mugas or flows on occasion, almost by accident. Although our database is small, we believe we can help Level 7 thinkers become better putters by adopting the BIRDMAN technique. Also when the BIRDMAN technique is used by the Level 7s, they have a tendency to be drawn into the activity, which lends itself to experiencing a *muga* or entrance into the zone.

The BIRDMAN process is explained in detail in Chapter 8. The important points to remember are

1. Imagine a sight on the barrel of a gun. Imagine this same sight six to ten inches from the ball directly on the aimline.

2. Mentally see the ball roll across the sight and hear it drop into the cup.

3. Feel the excitement of the holed putt.

4. Strike the ball.

When this process is used by the Level 7 brain what happens is there is a magnified explosion in the brain when the putt actually drops in the hole. What causes this magnified activation in the brain is first, the rear of the brain is fired when the ball is imagined going over the sight and then imagined dropping in the hole. As the conscious makes the unconscious fire, the ball is actually struck, and as it falls the rear of the brain explodes again but this time with more fire power. This fire power is so exciting that the putter wants to do it again and again.

Larry Bird, legendary basketball player, loved to practice. He would shoot baskets by himself hour after hour. Putting this in perspective, we see a millionaire shooting baskets tirelessly for the love of it.

After experiencing the BIRDMAN sight of the barrel technique, the Level 7 can amplify the firing even more by doing the following:

1. Never putting the ball the same distance twice in a row while practicing.

2. Using a different putter for each putt while practicing.

3. As the Level 7 approaches Zen status, using a different stroke while putting varying distances using different putters will blow the rear of the brain into the Fourth Dimension.

Only Level 7s will understand, appreciate, and benefit from this approach. All others will see it as weird.

Strengths

Intensity; focus; self-assurance; joy; contribute to the greater good

Weaknesses

Unwillingness to please; enjoys chaos and, at times, causes chaos; disruptive; too frank; too self-righteous

Improvement

Teach others; keep records on personal insights; say "I'm sorry" and "please"; be kind to those close to you; cheer down

Must Read

Murphy, M. (1972). *Golf in the kingdom*. New York: Penguin Books.

Any Level will find this book interesting and fun reading, but the Level 7 will see beyond the words printed on the page.

Chopra, D. (2003). *Golf for enlightenment*. New York: Harmony Books.

This will be interesting reading for a Level 7, but it won't help improve the Level 7s putting.

Parent, J. (2002). *Zen golf*. New York: Doubleday.

This book will stimulate some thinking and ideas about putting that are worth trying.

PeopleWise® Pattern Descriptions
LEVEL 4-5, ABSOLUTIST-MATERIALIST BLEND

Characteristics

You are the best of two worlds; solid work ethic coupled with the right amount of drive and desire. You are competitive, yet you play by the rules. Sportsmanship is important to you. You lead by your actions and deeds. People see you as healthy and purposeful. People admire your level headedness. You plan things and have the energy to carry out your plan. Sometimes you get caught in a dilemma; you want things done right, yet you want things done in a timely manner. Pushed to an extreme, you may, on occasion, want things done perfect, and you want things done immediately. These opposing drives place you in a predicament that forces excellence — top quality in breakneck speed. This dual drive, when mastered, places you head and shoulders above your peers and competitors. However, this dual drive, when unmastered, may occasionally lead to indecision, confusion, and possibly chaos. When you are unsure, you are best advised to slow down and make your decision based on your principles and standards. When in doubt, think things out. You might get some insights into yourself by studying the PeopleWise® Pattern Description of LEVEL 4, ABSOLUTIST and LEVEL 5, MATERIALIST. Keep in mind that you are a combination of both. You are able to take the best of both. One does not have to comprise the other.

Brain Activation

Your brain activates in both the right and left hemispheres. Skill improvement is best when you follow a two-phase process. First, you master the basics. This is done by focusing on proper positioning of your body and execution of the ideal, traditional muscle movement, i.e., proper stance and proper body movement. Once you master the basics without having to think, you move to the second phase, which is all mental. Here you focus on training your brain to visualize the outcome. Before execution, you first see in your "mind's eye" exactly the perfect outcome. Then you must feel what it is like to succeed. This feeling of success or accomplishment gives you confidence. After you feel the success, you actually begin execution of your skill movement. For you, first work the left side of the brain, mastering the basics. Then activate the right side of the brain through visualizing the outcome. To get a better grasp of the procedure, read and master the Basics section for LEVEL 4, ABSOLUTIST, then proceed to the Mind Control section and Peoplewise® Putting section for LEVEL 5, MATERIALIST found in the PeopleWise® Pattern Descriptions. Do not try the long-handled putter. You are going to move from practice makes perfect to perfect practice makes perfect.

Basics

As a Level 4-5, begin to grip the club as firm as a young baby grips your finger when trying to pull up or stand. Become aware of how you grip various objects like a cup or drinking glass. This is the pressure you want to develop for putting.

Place your head directly above the rear of the ball and keep it still throughout the putting stroke. With the baby's grip, it is important to hit the ball on the sweet spot. As always, keep the putterhead square to the aimline and the swing on the aimline path.

You will not have any difficulty lining the putt up to determine the aimline, but distance will remain a problem. When using the pendulum motion, regulate the length of the putt based on the length of the arc. Longer arc — longer putt, shorter arc — shorter putt. Keep the speed and rhythm of the swing the same. Only alter the length of the arc.

With the firmness of a baby's grip, you will feel a difference in your hands related to the distance as the putterhead strikes the ball. Feeling this slight difference in your hands will increase your sensitivity. As your sensitivity increases, you will train your subconscious to better judge distances. On the practice green, practice lagging putts to designated areas to develop a sensitivity that will improve the subconscious' ability to judge distance. As a left-right brainer you judge distance by mathematics and feel.

Get two putters you feel comfortable with and use them on alternating days. This begins to telegraph to your subconscious that you are more important then the putter. Do not try a long-handled putter because it will only confuse your mind.

Mind Control

With a Level 4-5, left-right brainer, it is best to use the left side of the brain for basics, but the basics must come naturally without thinking. Also, you must perfect hitting the ball on the sweat spot every time. When this is accomplished, you can begin to activate the right side of the brain by crafting a picture of yourself channeling the ball in the hole as opposed to mechanically striking it like a robot.

As you picture yourself channeling the ball in the hole, this heightens your sensitivity and stimulates more emotion. Your self-talk arouses three feelings in you: sensitivity, emotion and awareness. Since you don't have to worry about the basics you can begin to craft a picture of yourself as an architect who must be sensitive to the surroundings and the environment yet precise.

You talk yourself into picturing yourself constructing the perfect putt with computer precision. As the mental putts fall in digitized resolution, you generate excitement that builds confidence and pride. Your mind control will continue to be solidified as you practice PeopleWise® Putting using the TUBE technique. In other words, the Level 4-5 brain combines mind control with the TUBE technique of PeopleWise® Putting.

PeopleWise® Putting

For the Level 4-5 brain the TUBE is visualized as an architectural tunnel. As the architect of the tunnel, you are its creator. You have built the tunnel for the purpose of channeling golf balls into a receptacle.

Since you have created the tunnel, you automatically focus on the tunnel rather than the receptacle. By focusing on the tunnel, you have psychologically moved the cup closer because once the ball enters the tunnel it will automatically fall in the receptacle at the other end.

Your visual imagery of you, the architect, and your putting method of channeling the ball in the tunnel is so clear all you need to do is mentally see the ball enter the tunnel, hear the ball fall in the receptacle, get excited, and finally stroke the putt for real. After just a few successful trials, you will be tempted to strike the ball after mentally seeing the ball go in the tunnel. This defeats the purpose of firing the right side of the brain. What fires the right side of the brain is the excitement of hearing the imaginary putt fall in the receptacle after entering the tunnel. Do not try to rush this process or shorten it. You must get in the habit of striking the ball after, and only after you feel the excitement of the imaginary putt falling in the receptacle.

Once you begin to hit the ball consistently using the TUBE technique, start measuring your skill level. Use the information on Determining the Power of PeopleWise® Putting found at the end of Chapter 8. Find a level area on the practice putting green and mark a ten-foot distance in one-foot intervals by placing a tee each foot from the hole. Putt five balls at each of the one-foot distances and calculate your score. Do this five or six times.

When emotion is experienced prior to hitting the ball and since the hole is psychologically closer, the data convinces the subconscious to keep firing. As the firing continues, the putting stroke becomes more repeatable. The feedback measurement system moves what little practice you do from practice makes perfect to perfect practice makes perfect.

Your brain naturally fires on both the left and right sides. It will be a mistake to try to force your brain to fire on only one side because the subconscious will automatically make both sides fire. Since both sides fire you don't want them competing for dominance, so you merely assign rules for each side to play. In your case, the left brain's role is basics while the right brain's role is all mental. Assigning roles in this manner allows you to have the best of both worlds without compromising or competing with one another.

Strengths

Self-discipline; high energy; achievement; good follow through

Weaknesses

At times overdoes it; impulsive; sometimes over opinionated; impatient

Improvement

Become more visionary; listen more; try out new things; slow down

Must Read

Pelz, D. (2000). *Dave Pelz's putting bible*. New York: Doubleday.

There is more, much more in this book than you need. You need only Chapters 3, 5, 6 and 8.

Chapter 3 Methods of Putting

Chapter 5 Five Nonphysical Building Blocks: Touch, Feel, Attitude, Routine, and Ritual

Chapter 6 Stability and Rhythm: Two Artistic Fundamentals

Chapter 8 Speed is More Important than Line

These four chapters will help any Level 4-5 brainer, but Chapter 8 is essential. Remember, don't let the right side of the brain get overpowered by the left with mechanics, left = mechanics and right = mental. When the mind gets too caught up in the detail and trivia of the mechanics of putting, the right, which is analytical and calculative, may have a tendency to let the left which is simple and straight forward, dominate the thinking and putting process. Keep the basics simple, and let the right visualize and tabulate the results that will telegraph a repeatable stroke to the subconscious.

PeopleWise® Pattern Descriptions
LEVEL 5-6,
MATERIALIST-SOCIOCENTRIC BLEND

Characteristics

You are the best of two worlds: healthy drive and desire, coupled with the right amount of sensitivity. You get the job done with heart. Accomplishment is important, as are people's opinions and feelings. You have a knack for getting things done. You can lead by example, or you can convince people to do things by cheering them on from the sidelines. Winning is important but never more important than learning. You are into doing while, at the same time, being. You have a strong desire to assist people in their development, growth, and maturation while they are accomplishing a task or experiencing victory. You don't have much of a dilemma in your life because you have figured out winning is only as important as what is accomplished through winning. For you, winning is not a goal, winning is a process. You might get some insights into yourself by studying the PeopleWise® Pattern Description LEVEL 5, MATERIALIST and LEVEL 6, SOCIOCENTRIC. Keep in mind; you are a combination of both. You are able to take the best of both. One does not compromise the other but at the 5-6 Level when mastering a skill, it is best to use the calculative right side of the brain to heighten the front part of the brain, so your entire body, mind and soul become aware and attuned to the present moment. In other words, you use the right side of the brain to exploit the strengths of the frontal region of the brain.

Brain Activation

Your brain activates in both the right and front. Skill improvement is developing the "will" to make it happen. This is difficult because you have a tendency to want to run before you walk. You like to experiment and try things out. You are constantly questioning and experimenting. You are best advised to play around with your skill development. Read, study, get training video tapes or DVDs, and study different techniques and philosophies. Once you decide on the philosophy and technique you are going to use, begin to spend the majority of your time preparing for the mental part. Your brain activates on the right side, which is excellent for studying cause and effect. You have excellent analytical skills. You use the right side of the brain to determine which philosophy or technique is best for you. After the decision is made on what is best for you, you begin to activate the front part of the brain to get a feeling for what it is like to execute perfectly. By combining the right and front parts of the brain, you develop a "will" for perfection. This "will" for perfection can give you a competitive edge; however, this "will" can only be achieved through rigorous mental training. Without disciplined, rigorous training you have a tendency to see the activity for what it is, just a game. At this point your interest turns to enjoying the activity as opposed to mastering the skill. You use the game to experience life or to learn about yourself. True mastery comes from disciplined mental training, but it isn't easy. Read the sections on Brain Activation, Mind Control, and PeopleWise® Putting for LEVEL 5, MATERIALIST and LEVEL 6, SOCIOCENTRIC found in the PeopleWise® Pattern Descriptions. This may give you an insight into your complex self.

Basics

As a Level 5-6, your skill goes beyond basics and relies on experimentation utilizing touch, feel, sensitivity and rhythm. You are far from being regimented or mechanical. You calculate with awareness. You have your feet firmly planted on the ground, yet you can dream and imagine.

The basics will come to you through experimentation and awareness. Your first step to becoming a PeopleWise® putter is to select the right putter. One of your cognitive assets is you are not hung up on looks. You are interested in how the putter makes you feel, and you know that developing superior feel and touch are key to being a superior putter.

Get a variety of putters, and experiment with each of them over a three- to four-day period. Then select the top three, but one must be a traditional-length putter, one a short-length putter (or one you choke down on), and one a long-handled putter. Do not rush this process because the selection of the putter will form the foundation from which you will attain putting excellence.

Take the three putters and with all three begin to master the basics using the awareness technique. The awareness technique is explained in Chapter 3, Nuts and Bolts in the section Head Still. When working on keeping your head still, do not try to force it. Just become aware of what your head does during the stroking of the ball. The same awareness approach is used for hitting the ball on the sweet spot. Don't force yourself to hit it on the sweet spot. Just be acutely aware of where the ball hits the club face, and you will automatically begin to adjust.

Do not try to be aware of both of these basics simultaneously. First master the head still, then the sweet spot. Although you are a cognitive person and can multitask, the basics are best-mastered one at a time. Keep in mind each basic must be mastered with each of the three clubs. First master keeping the head still with the regular-shafted putter, then the short-shafted putter or one you choke down on and finally the long-shafted putter. Once you have mastered the head being kept still with all three putters using the awareness technique, you move to mastering hitting the ball on the sweet spot.

After mastering the head and sweet spot with the three putters, begin to perfect the pendulum stroke with the clubhead square to the aimline and the swing on the aimline path using the awareness technique. This is best and most quickly accomplished by using the eight-foot fishing line and two eyehooks trick. The eight-foot fishing line and the two eyehooks trick is explained in Chapter 3, Nuts and Bolts in the section Smooth Stroke.

Pick out a level spot on the practice green, and place one eyehook in the ground about an inch behind the hole while stringing the fishing line across the center of the cup, and place the other eyehook in the ground so the fishing line is taut and about five inches in the air parallel to the ground. Place the ball directly under the fishing line about two to three feet from the cup to begin with. Since you don't have to think about your head or sweet spot, focus your awareness on the squareness of the putterhead and the swing on the aimline path. Do not try to keep the putterhead square or the swing on line. Just become acutely aware of these directional basics as you stroke the ball. By using the eight-foot fishing line, two hooks aide you will immediately sense when you execute the stroke correctly. Again, do not force it. Let your complex mind engage with your senses, and you will quickly become one, with the basics, using the three clubs.

At this point your confidence level is at such a high pitch you will think you have attained excellence. Don't end your pursuit for being a PeopleWise® putter yet; move to Mind Control.

Mind Control

After selecting the three putters and mastering the basics using the awareness technique you can now focus on perfecting your picture. The creative subconscious can hone in on the image of being a perfect putter so the stroke becomes repeatable without conscious effort. For you, the Level 5-6 brainer, the picture is a world-class orchestra conductor. You begin to see yourself as the Maestro of the putting green. You use your putter as a baton conducting a symphony with an orchestra made up of ball, grass, and cup.

Your self-talk of words, picture, and emotion allows you to imagine yourself on stage (practice putting green) conducting a symphony, and as the ball and cup harmonize, you receive a standing ovation from the gallery. After every standing ovation, your stroke becomes more repeatable as you bask in the beauty and glory.

After mastering the basics using the awareness technique and visualizing yourself as a world-class orchestra conductor receiving standing ovation after standing ovation, you are ready to attain greatness by controlling the firing of your brain through PeopleWise® Putting.

PeopleWise® Putting

As a Level 5-6 brainer, you will begin to combine the TUBE technique with the FEEL-SEE-DO technique. As a world-class orchestra conductor, the TUBE changes length as volume changes in sound from the orchestra. As a conductor when you want more sound you raise your left hand while keeping the rhythm with the right. As a Maestro of putting, as you want more distance you mentally lengthen the TUBE while physically keeping the rhythm with the putter. The rhythm, the beat, stays the same. Physically the length of the arc changes, but the rhythm stays the same. Mentally the TUBE adjusts to the length of the putt; longer putt — longer TUBE — longer arc, shorter putt — shorter TUBE — shorter arc.

To help with determining the optimal length of the TUBE take two ball markers or two tees and place them in the ground the width of the cup at varying distances from the hole. Putt the ball between the markers/tees and experiment with what works best at your skill level depending on how far the ball is from the hole.

You have mastered the basics and mind control. Now you master TUBE length. Once you master TUBE length you are ready to use the FEEL-SEE-DO technique.

Everything you have done up to this point leads to the optimal attainment of FEEL-SEE-DO. FEEL is being acutely aware of everything simultaneously without force. You are aware of head still, sweet spot, pendulum swing, putterhead square, swing on aimline path, ball, cup, grass, gallery, and TUBE length. Now you SEE the ball submerge in the cup with harmony at which point you explode with pride and excitement as the gallery yells and jumps for joy after which you DO. You strike the ball.

You perfect the FEEL-SEE-DO approach with all three putters. Now you select your baton to use for the season.

You select the putter by measuring which one you putt with best. Use the information on Determining the Power of PeopleWise® Putting found at the end of Chapter 8. Find a level area on the practice green, and mark a ten-foot distance in one-foot intervals by placing a tee each foot from the hole. Putt five balls at each of the one-foot distances with each of the three putters and calculate the differences.

Pick the putter that you score with best and use it for the entire season. Next season start over from the beginning and select the putter that makes the best music, i.e. score the best.

Take a moment to think what you have done. You have used your calculative right brain to heighten your sensitivity and aware-ness and become attuned to the present moment, which fires the frontal region. The frontal region is so important to putting because it is the home of feeling and sensitivity. Feeling and sensitivity in putting are of paramount importance.

By using the right brain to heighten your sensitivity, you have removed it from competing with the front. In extreme cases, the right brain can think too much and sometimes at the wrong time. But by focusing the cognitive part of your brain on sensitivity and awareness, you have consciously moved all your brain power, your activation of the brain, to the front. This frontal activation propels you to excellence as a putter.

Strengths

High energy; sensitive; purposeful intentions; achievement

Weaknesses

Will settle for less; impulsive; impatient; at times appears confused

Improvement

Be proactive; study and listen more; master a physical skill; slow down

Must Read

Gallwey, W. T. (1998). *The inner game of golf*. New York: Random House.

This book will help your right brain understand where you are going and how to get there.

PeopleWise® Pattern Descriptions

LEVEL 4-6,
ABSOLUTIST-SOCIOCENTRIC BLEND

Characteristics

You are the best of two worlds; you possess a solid work ethic coupled with the right amount of sensitivity. You value standards, policies, and rules, yet you have a true feeling for people and how procedures affect people. You do things right, and at the same time, you do the right things. People admire your healthiness. As you plan things out, you constantly weigh how people will react. Yet, at the same time, you understand that for the organization to survive, things must move forward in a timely fashion. You are able to get things accomplished through people, but if necessary, you can roll your sleeves up and do it yourself. Sometimes you get caught in a dilemma — you want things done right; yet you want people to like what they do. Because you are psychologically very healthy, these opposing drives of getting things done with happy, contented people brings out the best in everyone. However, on occasion, these opposing drives may cause you to hesitate or delay an action. When you are unsure, you are best advised to consider the greater good or the contribution to the whole because healthy individuals are adaptable and realize things can't always go their way. As long as the decision is based on what is best for the greater good or whole, everything else will fall in place. You might get some insights into yourself by studying the PeopleWise® Pattern Description LEVEL 4, ABSOLUTIST and LEVEL 6, SOCIOCENTRIC. Keep in mind; you are a combination of both. You are able to take the best of both. One does not compromise the other.

Brain Activation

Your brain activates in both the left and front. Skill improvement is best when you follow a two-phase process. First, you master the basics. This is done by focusing on proper positioning of your body and execution of the ideal, traditional muscle movement, i.e. proper stance and proper body movement. Once you master the basics without having to think, you move to the second phase, which is all mental. Here you focus on training your brain to feel the rhythm. Before execution, you first imagine what it feels like to execute perfectly. This feeling of what it is like to be a champion builds confidence. Confidence is knowing you are good. For you, you first work the left side of the brain, mastering the basics. Then you activate the front of the brain through visualizing what it feels like to execute perfectly. To get a better grasp of the procedure, read and master the Basics section on LEVEL 4, ABSOLUTIST, then proceed to the Mind Control section and PeopleWise® Putting section on LEVEL 6, SOCIOCENTRIC, from the PeopleWise® Pattern Descriptions. You are going to move from practice makes perfect to feeling perfection.

Basics

As a Level 4-6, begin to grip the club as firm as a young baby grips your finger when trying to pull up or stand. Become aware of how you grip various objects like a cup or drinking glass. This is the pressure you want to develop for putting.

Place your head directly above the rear of the ball and keep it still throughout the putting stroke. With the baby's grip, it is important to hit the ball on the sweet spot. As always, keep the putterhead square to the aimline and the swing on the aimline path.

You will not have any difficulty lining the putt up to determine the aimline, but distance will remain a problem. When using the pendulum motion, regulate the length of the putt based on the length of the arc. Longer arc — longer putt, shorter arc — shorter putt. Keep the speed and rhythm of the swing the same. Only alter the length of the arc.

With the firmness of a baby's grip, you will feel a difference in your hands related to the distance as the putterhead strikes the ball. Feeling this slight difference in your hands will increase your sensitivity. As your sensitivity increases, you will train your subconscious to better judge distances. On the practice green, practice lagging putts to designated areas to develop a sensitivity that will improve the subconscious' ability to judge distance. As a left-front brainer, you judge distance by mathematics and feel.

Get two putters, one traditional putter with a traditional length shaft and one putter with the shaft four to six inches shorter. Do not try a long-handled putter because it will only confuse your mind and interfere with your rhythm and feel.

Determine which putter to use by measuring which one you putt best with. Use the information on Determining the Power of PeopleWise® Putting found at the end of Chapter 8. Find a level area on the practice green and mark a ten-foot distance in one-foot intervals by placing a tee each foot from the hole. Putt five balls at each of the one-foot distances with each of the putters and calculate the difference.

Pick the putter that you score with best and do not change. As a Level 4-6 you will become one with the putter even if at first it feels awkward or unfriendly. The important point is when selecting a putter as a Level 4-6 you select it based on brains rather than heart.

Mind Control

With a Level 4-6, left front brainer, it is important to use the left side of the brain for basics but the basics *must* come naturally without thinking. When you have mastered the basics of head still, sweet spot, pendulum stroke with the putterhead square, and the swing on the aimline path, you can begin to activate the front of the brain by giving the ball to the hole as opposed to mechanically striking it like a robot.

As you picture yourself giving the ball to the hole this gives you a frame of mind that you are letting things happen as opposed to forcing things to happen or manipulating the ball in any way. Since you don't have to worry about the basics, you begin to mold a picture of yourself as a human grandfather clock that is wise, kind, and giving. As a grandparent to the ball and hole, you bring them together.

You talk yourself into picturing yourself giving the ball to the hole with kindness and feeling. As the ball is received by the hole, you experience joy in the union. This repeated union generates ecstasy that builds pride and grand satisfaction. Your mind control will continue to nurture itself as you practice PeopleWise® Putting using the FEEL-SEE-DO approach. In other words the Level 4-6 brain combines mind control with the FEEL-SEE-DO approach of PeopleWise® Putting.

PeopleWise® Putting

For the Level 4-6 brain the FEEL-SEE-DO approach starts with a clear picture of you as a grandfather clock using a pendulum motion and giving the ball to the hole. Instead of the clock going "tick tock," you, as the grandfather clock, go "take me." As the club moves back you say to yourself "take," and as the club head moves forward you say to yourself "me." This tick tock — take me rhythm enhances your feeling and helps you attain a level of hypersensitivity.

The left side of the brain takes care of all the basics. This leaves the front area to totally dedicate itself to feel, awareness and sensitivity. From time to time, assume the position, stance and address without a ball, and merely move the club back and forth while saying "take me, take me, take me." Since you don't have to think about the basics, your feeling, awareness, and sensitivity will immediately swell within you.

On the practice green you address the ball then FEEL — the joy of giving the ball to the hole in a take me fashion. Then SEE

— the ball and hole unite, become one, at which time the front of your brain fires with joy and gratitude. Then you DO — by actually striking the ball as you actually say "take" on the back swing and "me" as the club head moves forward (some Level 4-6 brainers say "me" as the putterhead strikes the ball).

Because you are a Level 4-6, this approach is so powerful, so gratifying, and so effective that you will think the secret is in the "take me." Don't be seduced into the simplification of this type of thinking. The secret to getting your brain to activate in the frontal region is when the emotion, the joy, and gratitude are felt as you imagine the ball and hole uniting. Never actually stroke the ball until you feel the joy and gratitude. In fact, try to immediately start the back swing while simultaneously saying to yourself "take" as the feeling of joy and gratitude presents itself. The exact timing of feeling to taking away the clubhead with saying "take" is crucial but as a Level 4-6 when this does happen you will have a hard time containing your enthusiasm. In fact, as a Level 4-6, after reading this you will smile to yourself and think, "I get it." "This I can do and it will work." You will feel perfection.

Strengths

Reliable; sensitive; self-disciplined; purposeful intentions

Weaknesses

Resistant to change; indecisive at times; worrisome; lack direction at times

Improvements

Become more visionary; master a physical skill; try out new things; become proactive

Must Read

Gallwey, W.T. (1998). *The inner game of golf*. New York. Random House.

As you read this book, pay particular attention to the Back — Hit — Stop and the DA — DA — DA — DA techniques. They will give you insight on the "take me" technique. Keep in mind, this is a powerful technique, but feeling the joy and gratitude of mentally seeing the hole and ball unite before actually striking the ball is the secret to PeopleWise® Putting.

PeopleWise® Pattern Descriptions
LEVEL 4-7, LEVEL 5-7, LEVEL 6-7
COGNITIVE — DEVELOPING

Characteristics

You have had an opportunity to experience a lot of things in your life. You have had ups and downs, joy and sorrow, good and bad, fun and sad. However, the bad times invigorate you as much, if not more, than the good times. The world is coming at you from all directions, and you are loving it. You do a lot of thinking about life-death, right-wrong, legal-illegal, justice-injustice, and although you have opinions regarding these complex, ethical issues, you enjoy playing mental gymnastics by placing related situations in extreme conditions to test your opinion. You are growing into a person that is a paradox in action. You are internally driven and the sorrowful times, the bad times, the sad times are nothing more than opportunities and lessons.

You have a tendency to look back. Don't look back; the answer lies within. You are at a stage in life where you will take unnecessary risks that might place you in dangerous surroundings. You are unconsciously trying to conquer fear. You will leave this developing stage and arrive at totality when you conquer all fear. You are close to it now, but there still remains an area or two that you fear. Some fearful areas might include death, social rejection, poverty, criticism, torture, lack of respect, loneliness, etc.

You will eventually conquer fear completely. There is no way to reach totality without conquering fear completely; however, if you never conquer fear you are still way ahead of every one else. Remember, you are beyond winning; you are into "being."

Brain Activation

Your brain is firing in the rear, which dominates the other areas. The secret to your success in skill development is to use techniques, models and processes that accelerate rear-brain activation.

To control rear-brain activity, use the opportunity to master a skill that will help you get into the flow or zone. You presently get into the flow or zone periodically, but it is caused from an outside source rather than you causing it. You obviously have to practice a little, but do not spend an inordinate amount of time with the basics or analysis of the skill movement. Your best bet is to experiment with self-hypnosis or some type of meditation.

Study your internal self as opposed to the basics or movement analysis. As you get more and more in touch with your inner self, you will connect these inner feelings with the mastery of the skill itself.

The study of psycho-cybernetics might help, but you are capable of going beyond basic visual imagery and mental rehearsal. Yes, you must practice, but how you practice is very important. For you, perfect practice doesn't make perfect because you are destined to break existing barriers — break the mold, so to speak. So instead of practice, practice, practice, you meditate, practice, experiment, experience, meditate, practice, experiment, experience, meditate, practice, experiment, experience....

Basics

As a developing Level 7, your skill in putting lies in you getting in the zone or flow. For you, basics are to be experimented with, tested and played with. For you the basics change as you get new information about you, your putter, the ball, the green, and the situation.

Begin by studying the relationship of other sport skills to putting. Study things like shooting a basketball, hitting a tennis ball, playing pool, and even juggling. Read at least three different approaches to golf. If possible, go to some golf clinics or look at some training tapes/DVDs. Gradually your basic skills will formulate into a workable pattern.

Be aware that traditional instructional methods do not work for you. You do not learn from a step-by-step program moving from simple to complex. You also do not learn from a cause and effect procedure that is logical or theoretically based. Skill-awareness training is too affective for you at this time in your development.

You learn by the assimilation of globs of stuff that may seem unrelated, and suddenly your mind cracks the code with an insight or paradigm shift. Your mind works in bursts and is revolutionary not evolutionary.

You learn the basics by collecting vast amounts of information and then letting the magnificence of your mind sort it out. Do not rush the basics nor simplify them. When you sort it out it will be clear, logical, and simple to you, but remember your mind is very complex, and it can handle lots and lots of stuff simultaneously. To others your basics may seem odd or weird, but don't pay any attention to them. But of course you wouldn't anyway.

Mind Control

The more you understand the mind and how it develops the better. Definitely study some meditation techniques, self-hypnosis, and theories on the development of humankind. Look at work that has been done on understanding the flow or zone.

A good place to start would be *PeopleWise® Brain to Brain*, the first book in the PeopleWise® Series. Read the original works of Csikszentmihalyi, Graves, Maltz, Maslow, Tice, and Waitley. See the bibliography at the end of this book for titles.

After some reading and studying on how the mind works, your complex brain will sort out the system that works for you. Be aware that your system is fluid and will change as you gather new ideas, new information, new insights…You are constantly growing, and your mind is constantly expanding.

PeopleWise® Putting

As a developing Level 7, the key is using the BIRDMAN technique after you have learned to get into the flow. You may experience success with the BIRDMAN technique even prior to formulating the basics that work for you and even before you master mind control through visual imagery and mental rehearsal.

Your mind works all kinds of ways through different dimensions, but the BIRDMAN technique seems to be very effective for complex brains like yours at any time in the learning process. The BIRDMAN technique is explained in Chapter 8, PeopleWise® Putting in the section Rear Brain Dominant, Level 7, Cognitive and in the PeopleWise® Pattern Description Level 7, Cognitive under the section PeopleWise® Putting. The summary of the BIRDMAN process is as follows:

1. Imagine a sight on the barrel of a gun. Imagine this same sight six to ten inches from the ball directly on the aimline.

2. Mentally see the ball roll across the sight and hear it drop into the cup.

3. Feel the excitement of the holed putt.

4. Strike the ball.

Since your brain is at the developing stage, only use the first two steps in actual practicing, which are

1. Never putt the ball the same distance twice in a row while practicing.

2. Use a different putter for each putt while practicing.

Do not try step three until your brain moves totally to activating in the rear. You will know this when you can get into the zone on demand and you have conquered all fear. Once you become a zone master and you conquer fear, then, and only then, do you go to the third step and use a different stroke each time you putt a ball on the putting green.

As a Level 7 Cognitive Developing, you are not into doing — you are into being.

Strengths

Creativity; invention; experimentation; novelty; self-assurance

Weaknesses

Disruptive; distant; too frank; off the wall

Improvement

Be sincere; slow down; practice good body language; say, "thank you," "I'm sorry," and "please" often

Must Read

Parent, J. (2002). *Zen golf*. New York: Doubleday.

Along with the other readings suggested earlier, *Zen Golf* will be enough to get you started on the right foot.

EPILOGUE

I have dedicated a substantial portion of my life to studying, researching, applying, and developing the PeopleWise® program. PeopleWise® is more than a series of books. It is more than a set of methods, techniques, or tricks. I believe it is the future and, for a select few, can be used to create the future through post-living.

PeopleWise® has affected my thinking and altered my behavior. Rather than evolving or unfolding, PeopleWise® develops through jerks and abrupt twists that form mind bursts. These mind bursts are insights, ah-hahs, paradigm shifts, break-throughs, and breakwiths.

Each day, each week, each month, each year PeopleWise® becomes more and more clear. PeopleWise® is too important to keep a secret, it is too important to keep to ourselves. Larry and I want you to share your thoughts with us. All comments, suggestions, questions and ideas are welcome.

James S. Payne
Management and Motivation, Inc.
P O Box 215
University, MS 38677
1-800-514-7626
FAX#: (662) 281-8780
mm@watervally.net

www.managementandmotivation.com

Definition of Terms

Address — How a player stands to get ready to hit the ball.

Aimline — The initial line that the ball is intended to start on.

Birdie — One stroke under par.

Break — The distance between the aimline and the hole. For instance, on a two-inch break the ball moves two inches from the intended aimline to the hole, i.e. it breaks two inches.

Bogey — One stroke over par.

Fairway — The playing area identified with short grass from the tee to the green.

Foursome — A group of four players.

Green in Regulation (GIR) — The number of strokes identified as the number needed to get on the green when playing every shot correctly. On par four holes the GIR is two. On par five holes the GIR is three. On par three holes the GIR is one.

Green Speed — See Stimpmeter

Handicap —   A number decided by a formula of how well a
                    player plays as it relates to par. The number is
                    used to equalize the contest. When actually
                    figured the handicap is a weighted mean.
                    Out of the most recent twenty scores, the ten
                    highest are eliminated. Ninety-six percent of
                    the average of the lowest ten scores results in
                    being the handicap. A legitimate 18 handicap
                    should only score 90 (72 par + 18 = 90) 20
                    percent of the time yielding an equivalent score
                    of par (90 - 18 = 72 par). The remaining 80
                    percent of the time the scores should be higher
                    than par, that is more than 90.

Heel —   The inside portion of the face of the putterhead.

Mulligan —   A player is given an extra shot and the best of
                    two shots, is selected to be played without
                    penalty.

Par —   The number of strokes identified as the number
                    needed when doing everything correctly.

Practice Green —   A green, usually next to the clubhouse,
                    designed for practicing putting. It has multiple
                    cups so several players can practice putting at
                    the same time.

Putterface —   The side of the putter that strikes the ball.

Qualifying School — A place where it is determined what players
                    are eligible to play professionally on tour.

Reading the Greens — Studying everything that might affect the
                    direction and distance of the putt. Examples
                    include undulation, length of the grass,
                    moisture on the green, grain of the grass, etc.

Rough —	The area next to the fairway that has longer grass.
Scramble —	When two or more players play the best ball after each has hit. For instance, four players all hit their drives off the tee. They select the best shot of the four that they want to play. The remaining three get their balls and place their balls next to the one to be played. This is continued until a ball is holed. A team score is recorded of the total of the best ball. A Scramble is sometimes called a Superball or Bestball.
Single Digits —	An established handicap of one to nine.
Sole —	The underneath side of the putterhead.
Square —	The perpendicular position of the putterhead to the aimline.
Stimpmeter —	A device developed by Edward Stimpson to determine how fast the ball rolls on a green. A slow green is about a seven. A fast green is about a ten. Most professional tournaments try for green speeds of ten and a half to eleven.
Sweet Spot —	The place on the putterface where contact feels the most solid, which eliminates all rotation and wobble on contact with the ball. It is technically referred to as the center of percussion.
Tee Time —	The time established for the player(s) to begin play.
Toe —	The outside portion of the face of the putterhead.
Undulating —	The hills and valleys on the putting surface.

USGA —   United States Golf Association. The official golf
           association of the United States that serves as the
           governing body.

Bibliography

Andrisani, J. (1998). *The short game magic of Tiger Woods*. New York: Three Rivers Press.

Armour, T. (1953). *How to play your best golf all the time*. New York: Simon & Schuster.

Armour, T. (1967). *Tommy Armour's ABC's of golf*. New York: Simon & Schuster.

Balata, B. (1999). *Being the ball*. Phoenix: B. & B. Entertainment.

Bartlett, J. (1996). *Golf gurus: The wisdom of the game's greatest instructors*. Dallas: Taylor Publishing Co.

Chopra, D. (2003). *Golf for enlightenment*. New York: Harmony Books.

Coffee, G. (1990). *Beyond survival*. Aiea, Hawaii: Coffee Enterprises.

Cohn, P. J., & Winters, R. K. (1995). *The mental art of putting*. South Bend, IN: Diamond Communications, Inc.

Covey, S. R. (1989). *The 7 habits of highly effective people*. New York: Simon & Schuster.

Crosby, D. (2000). *Tiger Woods made me look like a genius*. Kansas City, MO: Andrews McMeel Publishing.

Csikszentmihali, M. (1998). *Finding flow: The psychology of engagement with everyday life*. New York: HarperCollins.

Diamond, M., & Hopson, J. (1998). *Magic trees of the mind: How to nurture your child's intelligence, creativity, and healthy emotions from birth through adolescence*. New York: Penguin Putnam.

Dobereiner, P. (1991). *Golf a la carte: The best of Dobereiner.* Short Hills, NJ: Burford Books, Inc.

Frankl, V. E. (1959). *Man's search for meaning.* New York: Simon & Schuster.

Gallwey, W. T. (1998). *The inner game of golf.* New York: Random House.

Glover, D. (1998). *Math like you've never seen it before* (videotape). Pittsburgh: WQED.

Goleman, D. (1995). *Emotional intelligence: Why it can matter more than I.Q.* New York: Bantam.

Graves, C. W. (1996). The deterioration of work standards. *Harvard Business Review,* 44, 117-126.

Graves, C. W. (1970). Levels of existence: An open system theory of values. *Journal of Humanistic Psychology,* 10, 131-155.

Graves, C. W. (1974). Human nature prepares for a momentous leap. *The Futurist,* 8, 72-87.

Hogan, B. (1998). *Golf gadgets.* New York: Macmillan Publishing Co.

Kotulak, R. (1996). *Inside the brain: Revolutionary discoveries of how the mind works.* Kansas City, MO: Andrews & McMeely.

LeDoux, J. (1996). *The emotional brain: The mysterious under-pinnings of emotional life.* New York: Simon & Schuster.

Maltz, M. (1967). *Psycho-cybernetics.* New York: Prentice Hall.

Maslow, A. H. (1968). *Toward a psychology of being.* Princeton, NJ: Van Nostrand.

Maslow, A. H. (1971). *The farther reaches of human nature.* New York: Viking Press.

Mayer, W. E. (1957). *Brainwashing ... The ultimate weapon* (audio tape and transcription source unknown).

Miller, L. (1996). *Golfing in the zone.* New York: MJF Books.

Morrice, P. (2000). *The golf magazine putting handbook.* New York: The Lyons Press.

Murphy, M. (1972). *Golf in the kingdom.* New York: Penguin Books.

Parent, J. (2002). *Zen golf.* New York: Doubleday.

Payne, J. S. (2003). Unpublished proposal for, *PeopleWise® motivation: The art of motivating brain to brain.* Oxford, MS: Management and Motivation, Inc.

Payne, J. S. (2004). *PeopleWise® brain to brain.* Pittsburgh, PA: SterlingHouse Publisher, Inc.

Peck, M. S. (1999). *Golf and the spirit.* New York: Harmony Books.

Pelz, D. (2000). *Dave Pelz's putting bible.* New York: Doubleday.

Tice, L. E. (1989). *A better world, a better you.* New Jersey: Prentice Hall.

Waitley, D. (1983). *Seeds of greatness.* New York: Pocket Books.

About the Authors
Larry Wagster and Jim Payne

James S. Payne is a Fulbright Scholar and presently serves as professor of Special Education at the University of Mississippi. Dr. Payne is a nationally recognized speaker, trainer, and writer. He has written over fifteen textbooks, three of which were the largest selling texts in special education. He has consulted with many organizations like South Central Bell, Federal Express, Dover Elevators, Washington Redskins, Caterpillar, City Government of Beverly Hills, HealthSouth, Virginia Power, People's Bank, and Federal Reserve Bank. Dr. Payne was granted the official trademark for PeopleWise® from the United States Patent Office in 2001. The first book in the PeopleWise® Series, *PeopleWise® Brain to Brain* was published in 2004. Dr. Payne developed the PeopleWise® Event Management System, a superior time management program, and the PeopleWise® Profile System, a self-scoring instrument that helps individuals understand themselves and others.

Larry Wagster is the former Ole Miss golf coach. In 1961 he received his undergraduate degree in business administration from The University of Mississippi and served in the United States Marine Corps (active duty) from 1961 to 1965. He was the assistant golf pro at OJAI Valley Inn and Country Club in Ojai, California and Stardust Country Club in San Diego, California. He was the women's golf coach for The University of Mississippi from 1989 to 1991 and the men's golf coach in 1992 and 1993. In 1989, he won the Mississippi Senior State Amateur Championship, was a 1997 Medalist at the Mississippi Qualifying site for the United States Golf Association Senior Amateur, and was a qualifier for the match play portion of the USGA Senior Amateur. For 21 years, Mr. Wagster served as a special agent for the Federal Bureau of Investigation.